DEVIL's ADVOCATE: "But the average reader still can't understand the right-hand versions."

GURU: "But most of us usually aren't writing for average readers. Engineers and scientists write to other engineers and scientists, and so on. When we do write for lay readers, then of course we must avoid (or define) words they don't know—if we care to be understood. That's the only difference. ALWAYS REMEMBER: When all else fails, try English." Good, old-fashioned, plain English.

Medical Writing

This . . .
Prior to admission the subject was administering NPH insulin, between 18 and 25 units on a daily basis, and on the initial day of admission was rehydrated through the utilization of forced fluids, normal saline with 5% dextrose and water, with subsequent augmentation of potassium supplement due to hypokalemia. On the above regimen the patient's condition improved and subsequent feeding initially included full liquids, subsequently 1,500-calorie diabetic diet. The subject also during this admission experienced the aspiration of a thin bloody secretion via the nasogastric tube, indicated by a subsequent upper G.I. series to be associated with a sliding hiatus hernia without evidence of reflux or esophagitis.

. . . Means This:
Before admission the patient was taking between 18 and 25 units of insulin daily. On the day of admission she was rehydrated with forced fluids, normal saline with 5% dextrose and water. Later we added potassium supplement to relieve hypokalemia. The patient's condition improved on this regimen, and we began feeding her full liquids, then a 1,500-calorie diabetic diet. Also during this admission, the patient aspirated a thin bloody secretion through the nasogastric tube. An upper G.I. series showed a sliding hiatus hernia without evidence of reflux or esophagitis.

Writing Process 2000

by Albert Joseph

Prentice Hall
Upper Saddle River, New Jersey 07458

Library of Congress Cataloging-in-Publication Data
Joseph, Albert.
Writing process 2000 / by Albert Joseph.
p. cm.
Parts of this book have been previously published as Put it in writing by International Writing Institute, Inc., Cleveland, Ohio. —t.p. verso.
Includes index.
ISBN 0-13-441916-2
1. English language—Rhetoric. I. Title.
PE1408.J885 1996
808′.042—dc20 95-41914
CIP

Acquisitions Editor: *Elizabeth Sugg*
Production Editor: *Virginia Carroll*
Production Liaison: *Eileen M. O'Sullivan*
Director of Manufacturing & Production: *Bruce Johnson*
Manufacturing Manager: *Ed O'Dougherty*
Production Manager: *Mary Carnis*
Cover design: *Miguel Ortiz*
Text composition/design: *Selena R. Chronister*
Formatting/page make-up: *North Market Street Graphics*
Printer/Binder: *Banta-Harrisonburg*

Parts of this book have been previously published as *Put It In Writing* by International Writing Institute, Inc.—Cleveland, Ohio.

Printed in the United States of America

10 9 8 7 6 5 4 3 2 1

ISBN 0-13-441916-2

Prentice-Hall International (UK) Limited, *London*
Prentice-Hall of Australia Pty. Limited, *Sydney*
Prentice-Hall Canada Inc., *Toronto*
Prentice-Hall Hispanoamericana, S.A., *Mexico*
Prentice-Hall of India Private Limited, *New Delhi*
Prentice-Hall of Japan, Inc., *Tokyo*
Simon & Schuster Asia Pte. Ltd., *Singapore*
Editora Prentice-Hall do Brasil, Ltda., *Rio de Janeiro*

TO DYLENE, whose good-natured wisdom launched this work and kept it on track, and to the students who taught me things I now share with unknown friends.

Special thanks to Sharon A. Shelley, International Writing Institute, for editorial assistance, and to Zarina M. Hock, National Council of Teachers of English, for research on some difficult points.

There are no special kinds of writing . . .

"You've got to look at it this way: There is only one English language, and (with the exception of poetry) the principles for using it effectively are the same, regardless of the subject. In that sense, there are no special kinds of writing. There is just writing. And the language principles that make it easy to read and understand are the same—regardless of the subject."

—FROM CLASSROOM DISCUSSION

Contents

PART 1 (ON CLARITY)

Chapter 1: Clarity—Your First Objective 3

What Style Clothing Should Your Writing Wear?
The Major Problem
Speed
Image
Why People Write That Way

Chapter 2: Six Principles of Clear Writing 9

Principle 1: Prefer Clear, Familiar Words
Principle 2: Keep Most Sentences Short and Simple

Chapter 3: Six Principles of Clear Writing (continued) 33

Principle 3: Prefer Active Voice Verbs; Avoid Passives
Principle 4: Refer to People in Your Writing
Principle 5: Use Conversational Style as a Guide
Principle 6: Revise, Revise, . . . and Revise Again

Chapter 4: Changing Some Old Attitudes 51

The Three Taboos
How Important Is Brevity?

Chapter 5: Measuring Readability 67

The Reading Process
How the Experts Measure
Evaluating Your Own Writing
On Official Tone
On Legal Writing
On Scientific Writing

81 **Chapter 6: Guidelines for Nonsexist Writing**

The Infamous Generic *He*
Other *Man* Words
Job Descriptions
Male Bosses and Female Secretaries
About *Ms.*

PART 2 (ON ORGANIZING)

94 **Chapter 7: Power to the Reader**

Learning Power
The Inverted Pyramid Structure
The Five W's of Journalism
A Recommended Format for Formal Reports
A Checklist for Organizing

119 **Chapter 8: Sense and Nonsense about Planning (Pre-Writing)**

How to Outsmart the Deadline
The Importance of the False Start
Mapping the Trip
The Real Way to Outline

135 **Chapter 9: Finishing Touches of the Pros**

Headings: Readers Love Them
The Importance of White Space
Paragraph Structuring
Where Should Graphics Go?
Ways to Add Emphasis (Italics, Boldface, Bullets)
Fact and Fancy about Letters
About Dictation

147 **Chapter 10: Reviewing and Editing the Writing of Others**

149 **Chapter 11: What Computers Can and Can't Do for Writers**

PREFACE

THE TWO COMMANDMENTS of writing, I believe, must be: *Think Clearly,* and *Write Clearly.* If there must be a third, it should be: Neither of these is very useful without the other. Beyond these, if the creator of writing commandments were to grace us with a fourth, it almost certainly should be: Make reading an important part of your life; good habits will rub off on you.

Critical thinking and sensible use of the English language, then, are the ingredients of good writing; they are The Writing Process.

This book deals with the latter, the *language* part of writing.

What is a writer? Not just novelists and journalists need writing skills. You are a writer whenever you write something—whether it's a report, or advice to a friend, or a letter to a company that charged you for a statue of an Alaskan moose you did not buy. Although language skills alone will probably not win the day for you (you must first of all have a message worth stating), making your point effectively will empower your position. Conversely, poor expression makes it easy for people to reject or ignore your position, even when you are right. The power of the pen—or word processor—IS mighty. That surprises most students, but it's true. Ask the people who have been where you want to be.

It is often said, "Some people are born writers." Well, maybe. Some people might be born with that rare imaginative mind that allows them to *create* stories, or plotlines, that grip us and hold us spellbound. This is the *art* of writing. But almost anyone can learn the *language skills* part well enough to write effectively, with little difficulty. This is the *craft* of writing.

I most certainly take issue with the cliché, attributed [wrongly] to Marshall McLuhan a generation ago, "The medium is the message."* They are quite separate. Especially, you must deal separately with your message *and* the process of conveying it to your reader.

I have often advised would-be professional writers: Don't try to say things brilliantly; *try to say brilliant things.* It is the message that matters. Herman Melville, author of *Moby Dick,* said, "To produce a mighty book you must produce a mighty theme." How true that is; those who go to New York relying on writing style alone end up in other professions.

This book contains little that is new about writing.

What is new about *Writing Process 2000* is the rearrangement of priorities. This book deals entirely with the second part of the process—HOW you write,

*The title is *The Medium is the Massage* (not *Message*). McLuhan and co-author Quentin Fiore observed that societies have always been influenced more by the technology of the medium than by the content of its message.

not WHAT you write—skills such as choosing the right words, building them into a smooth flow of readable sentences, and organizing your information in the order that best helps your reader to understand and to deal intelligently with that information. These are the things writers *and readers* must deal with if knowledge is to be communicated successfully from writerbrain to readerbrain—from senderbrain to receiverbrain. Writers *encode* (send); readers *decode* (receive). To a large extent, the sender determines how well the receiver will receive.

Dare we define language as a tool for transporting information? If not, for what other purpose do cultures create language? Beauty? Of course. No other beauty, however, can exceed that of bringing knowledge to people everywhere—conveying as much information as possible, as accurately and clearly as possible, to as many people as possible. We can have this universal gift, fortunately, with no sacrifice of the other wondrous beauties of language.

May writing contribute to the fullness of your life.

—AMJ

About the Author

Albert Joseph is president of International Writing Institute and has almost certainly taught more people how to write than any other educator or writer who ever lived. He is the author of *Put It In Writing*, the most widely used writing course in the English-speaking world; *Executive Guide to Grammar*, a self-study reference guide; and *English 2000*, a companion piece to this book, and has been described as ". . . the most vocal of a small band of pioneering educators crusading for clear, readable English." He believes that anything written—whether a government regulation or a great novel—should be understandable.

For a large part of his life Mr. Joseph was editor-in-chief of a national business magazine. He has also been a member of the faculty of Case Western Reserve University and guest lecturer at several other universities, and for 11 years was writing consultant to the United States Central Intelligence Agency.

He first received national acclaim for his approach to teaching writing when his course was produced as a videotaped series by the National Educational Television Network. He is also author of *The New English*, an experimental course in English composition for eighth grade. He is former chairman of the board of directors of Plain Talk, Inc., a public interest group promoting the use of plain English in business and government documents.

"Restricting knowledge to a small group deadens the spirit and leads to spiritual poverty."

—Albert Einstein

INTRODUCTION

This collection of information has one goal: to help improve the writing skills of people everywhere.

Its principles should help ordinary people (that is, people who write things but are not professional writers) to write clearly—so clearly that the reader cannot possibly misunderstand the message. You may also be able to write faster—*much* faster in many cases—without wasting time fumbling over false starts and rewrites. And you will also know how to present your valuable ideas in a tone that pleases the reader and presents a pleasant, dignified image of the writer.

Furthermore, you should achieve these goals with no sacrifice in the accuracy, dignity, or detail of *what* you write.

Your writing may also gain considerable beauty, if you care about that, because the same characteristics of language that make writing clear also give it beauty. In addition, the principles should help you become a better reader, speaker, and listener. Especially your reading skill should improve, for understanding how to recognize and analyze writing weaknesses will surely help you overcome those weaknesses as you read.

The information is divided into two parts. Part 1 is on Clarity. It presents six well-established principles of clear writing. We will also explode some widespread taboos—bad advice about writing that you probably learned some time in your life. Nonsexist language, an important and relatively new consideration, is also discussed in detail. And you will be introduced to a simple procedure to measure how easy (or difficult) your writing is to read.

Part 2 is on Organizing. It explains ways of arranging the things you write in the order that best helps the reader to receive and understand as much information as possible, as quickly and accurately as possible. *Always the reader.* It also presents new (and surprisingly effective) outlining strategies that take advantage of, rather than oppose, the way your brain operates as it tries to construct logical flow during the writing process. No longer should writers need to fumble over false starts and waste time getting started. Part 2 also deals with important mechanical considerations that can, but needn't, puzzle writers—arranging the information on the pages in ways that best help the reader. Again, *always the reader; he or she is the only reason we write.*

"Thinking is the process of simplifying the relationships between ideas. Therefore, simplicity is not only desirable—it is the mark of the thinking person."

—ALBERT JOSEPH

Albert Joseph's instructional techniques have been used to train thousands of employees from these companies:

Accounting

Deloitte & Touche
Ernst & Young
Price Waterhouse

Chemical

Dow Chemical U.S.A.
Dubois Chemical Company
E.I. du Pont de Nemours & Co.
Hoechst Celanese
ICI Americas
Phillips Chemical Company
Stauffer Chemical Company

State Governments

State of California
State of Colorado
State of Connecticut
State of Delaware
State of Florida
State of Michigan
State of Nevada
State of New York
State of Ohio
State of Oklahoma
State of Tennessee

Construction

Bechtel Power Company
C-E Lummus Combustion Engineering, Inc.
Harza Engineering, Inc.
Research Cottrell

Financial Institutions

Barnett Bank
Chase Manhattan Bank
Comptroller of the Currency
Crocker Bank
Federal Intermediate Credit Banks
Federal Reserve Banks
Home Savings of America
Maryland National Bank
Merchants National Bank and Trust
Society Corporation
Union Bank and Trust

High Technology

Boeing Commercial Airplane Company
Digital Equipment Corporation
E-Systems
General Dynamics
Hughes Aircraft Company
IBM Corporation
ISC Systems Corporation
Lockheed Corporation
Martin Marietta Corporation
Northrop Corporation
Rockwell International Corporation
3M
TRW, Inc.
Unisys
United Technologies
Xerox Corporation

Health Care

Humana Incorporated
Kaiser Permanente
Kettering Medical Center
U. of Rochester Medical School

Insurance

Alexander & Alexander, Inc.
AMEX Life Assurance Co.
Blue Cross/Blue Shield Association
CIGNA
CNA Insurance Companies
Continental Insurance Company
Erie Insurance Group
Equitable Life Assurance Society
Farm Bureau Mutual Insurance Company
Farmer's Insurance Group
Government Employees Insurance Company
Insurance Services Office
Liberty Mutual Insurance
Metropolitan Life Insurance Companies
Mutual of Omaha
Nationwide Insurance Company
Northwestern Mutual Life Insurance Company
Ohio Casualty Group

Prudential Insurance Company
Sentry Insurance
The Travelers Companies
U.S. Insurance Group
Wausau Insurance Company

Manufacturing

British-American Tobacco Company
Brown & Williamson Tobacco Corporation
Caterpillar Incorporated
Chrysler Corporation
Eastman Kodak Company
Eaton Corporation
Ford Motor Company
General Electric
General Motors Corporation
Gillette Company
B.F. Goodrich Company
Johnson Wax
Lever Brothers Company
Lubrizol Corporation
Mason and Hanger-Silas Mason Company, Inc.
Owens-Corning Fiberglas
Phelps-Dodge Corporation
Premier Industries
Procter & Gamble Company
Timken Company
U.S. Steel Corporation
Westinghouse Electric Corporation
Zenith Corporation

Petroleum

Amerada Hess Corporation
Amoco Production Company
Arco Chemical Company
BP America
Chevron U.S.A.
Exxon Corporation
Imperial Oil Company, Ltd.
Marathon Oil Company
Mobil Oil Corporation
Phillips Petroleum Company
Shell Oil Company
Texaco, Inc.
UNOCAL

Pharmaceutical

Ayerst Laboratories, Inc.
Janssen Pharmaceutica
Miles Laboratories, Inc.
Pfizer, Inc.
G.D. Searle Consumer Products
Sterling Drug Incorporated

Telecommunication

AT&T Communications
AT&T Information Systems
AT&T Technologies
American Telephone & Telegraph Company
Ameritech
Bell Atlantic
Bell Laboratories
Bell Telephone Company of Canada
MCI Telecommunications
New York Telephone Company
NYNEX

U.S. Government

Bureau of Alcohol, Tobacco & Firearms
Central Intelligence Agency
Department of Agriculture
Department of the Army
Department of Labor
Department of the Navy
Department of Veterans Affairs
Fannie Mae
Federal Judicial Center
Internal Revenue Service
National Aeronautics & Space Administration
National Science Foundation
Social Security Administration
United States Air Force
United States Coast Guard

Utilities

Boston Edison Company
Central Hudson Gas and Electric Corporation
Columbia Gas Company
Commonwealth Edison Company
Detroit Edison Company
Duquesne Light Company
Eastern Utilities Associates
Georgia Power Company
Gulf States Utilities
Idaho Power Company
Louisiana Power & Light
Metropolitan Edison Company
Northeast Utilities
Ohio Edison Company
Pennsylvania Power Company
San Diego Gas and Electric
Union Electric Company

Others

ARA Institutional Services
BBDO, Inc.
Coca-Cola USA
Del Monte Corporation
Drexel Burnham Lambert
Hallmark Cards, Inc.
Heinz USA
A.T. Kearney, Inc.
Kerr-McGee Coal Corporation
Miami Herald Publishing Co.
Miller Brewing Company
North American Van Lines
Orlando Sentinel Star
JCPenney Company
Rubbermaid, Inc.
Saks Fifth Avenue
Sears Roebuck & Co.
Trane Company
United Airlines
Walt Disney World
Willis Corroon
Zayre Corporation

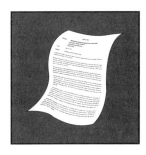

PART I
On Clarity

CLARITY—YOUR FIRST OBJECTIVE

- What Style Clothing Should Your Writing Wear?
- The Major Problem
- Speed
- Image
- Why People Write That Way

SIX PRINCIPLES OF CLEAR WRITING

- Principle 1: Prefer Clear, Familiar Words
- Principle 2: Keep Most Sentences Short and Simple

SIX PRINCIPLES OF CLEAR WRITING (*continued*)

- Principle 3: Prefer Active Voice Verbs; Avoid Passives
- Principle 4: Refer to People in Your Writing
- Principle 5: Use Conversational Style as a Guide
- Principle 6: Revise, Revise, . . . and Revise Again

CHANGING SOME OLD ATTITUDES

- The Three Taboos
- How Important Is Brevity?

"If a nation expects to be ignorant and free in a state of civilization, it expects what never was and never will be."

—Thomas Jefferson

CHAPTER 1

Clarity—Your First Objective

> In any communication the principal characters are a sender and a receiver. The idea being communicated exists in the sender's brain as electrical energy, not words, and if communication succeeds, that idea will end up in the receiver's brain as electrical energy. But we cannot transmit it that way, so we convert the idea from electricity to words and sentences. (Linguists call this process *encoding.*) These are easy to transport, written or spoken. But they exist just for the transportation. The receiver's brain, of course, must convert those black marks on a page, or those bits of sound, back to electrical impulses. (Reading experts call this process *decoding.*) Comprehension follows.

Your success as a writer, then, depends on your ability to choose words and build them into sentences that will cause the reader to receive the message you intended, accurately and clearly.

The French philosopher René Descartes (pronounced Day-cart´) is best known for expressing, in a few simple words, this profound and abstract thought: "*I think, therefore I exist.*" (Latin: "*Cogito, ergo sum.*") What a powerful lesson on how to communicate. Others might have written: "*The cognitive process presupposes the existence of the cognitive source.*" And no one would ever hear of it again. The writer's language usage can deprive readers of the message.

What Style Clothing Should Your Writing Wear?

Philip Dormer Stanhope, the Earl of Chesterfield, said of writing, "*Style is the dress of thoughts.*"

Compare writing styles to the styles of clothing we wear. We may own tank tops and jeans, and at the other extreme tuxedos or formal gowns. But in normal, everyday activities most of us wear something between those; either of those extremes would hurt our image. Likewise, there can be extremes in the language style we use to convey our thoughts to others.

Street talk and slang, the linguistic equivalent of tank tops and jeans, are helpful to most of us—and personally satisfying—when we use them at the right time and in the right place. Likewise, extremely formal and scholarly language should be used with enthusiasm in environments where and when that is expected. But in most writing situations neither of those extremes is helpful—and either one may be harmful. As with clothing, moderate taste will open most doors.

The Major Problem

The first thing we ask of the language is *clarity*—that it transport your ideas clearly, accurately, and efficiently—so that the message received is the one that was sent. Of course, we can also paint beautiful word pictures with language. Or we can create mood. But those goals are secondary. The only purpose for which cultures *create* language is to transport ideas. Then it is this simple: We cannot afford a transportation system that damages its cargo in transit. **You have done your job as a writer, as the sender in the communications link, when your ideas are so clear that your reader, the receiver, cannot possibly misunderstand them.**

Most adults have a tendency to overcomplicate during the writing process. Perhaps this happens because they do not really know (nobody ever taught them) how to write, or more specifically, what they are trying to achieve when they write. They try to sound as scholarly as possible. The thought process may be something like this: "*I'm an adult. Children use small words and short sentences, so I should do the opposite.*" In doing so, they may destroy the ideas they are trying to transmit.

Here is an example of what can go wrong as a result. This is what we mean when we say readers do not receive ideas accurately when writers use an overcomplicated style. This is an actual policy statement from the files of a government agency:

> Technical assistance to institutional administrative staffs is authorized in determination of the availability and appropriate utilization of federal and state entitlements designating assistance in resolution of problems occasioned by requirements of handicapped children. (33 words)

What does that say? Here is what the author meant:

> We can help your staff determine if federal or state funds are available to help meet the needs of handicapped children. We can also help you plan how best to use those funds. (33 words)

But it's not likely any reader would receive that message, no matter how hard he or she tries. The transportation system has delivered its cargo in unrecognizable condition. The original passage may sound dazzling, but it does not communicate; an important idea is broadcast but not received.

That is not enough. Communication does not take place until the idea has been received—and, furthermore, received *accurately*—and your job as a writer is to do whatever is necessary to *be* received accurately.

BUT CAUTION: Oversimplification is equally damaging. Your writing is *over*simplified when you leave out important information, or when simple words make a statement inaccurate, or when it sounds childish. We certainly wouldn't want that government memo to read:

> We can help you get government money. And we can help you spend it.

Whether overcomplicated or oversimplified, when we use language improperly the reader may receive some message other than the one we intended to send. Thoughtful writers are constantly aware this can happen and work hard to prevent it.

Speed

The second benefit of healthy writing habits is *speed* of the communication process. Most people take far too much time to write. That complicated style slows you down. Examine this passage from a company memo:

> . . . from other cities in advance. All meetings will be in the conference room except Tuesday, June 28, which will be in the main cafeteria. Management has become cognizant of the necessity for the elimination of undesirable vegetation surrounding the periphery of our facility. (19 words)

Compare that with what the writer really intended to say:

> . . . from other cities in advance. All meetings will be in the conference room except Tuesday, June 28, which will be in the main cafeteria. Please kill the weeds around the building. (7 words)

Although this example is exaggerated, the overcomplicated style usually uses about twice as many words as necessary—sometimes even more. This means twice as many words you must put on paper. Whether you write them longhand, dictate, type your own, or enter them into a computer, twice as many words means twice as long getting them recorded. Then consider this: Words like "*Management has become cognizant of the necessity for the elimination of undesirable vegetation surrounding the periphery of our facility*" do not come naturally; the writer must sit and wrestle with the words and with the sentences he or she will construct of them.

But again, that meant "*Please kill the weeds around the building.*" Those words come naturally; they are easy to write.

For those two reasons, then—the extra words and the extra time it takes to structure them into complicated, difficult sentences—language more complex than necessary slows down the writing process for misguided writers who shun simplicity. The writer, by comparison, who can express his or her thoughts in plain English has the distinct advantage of finishing quickly and going on to other things. This is the second gain that sensible language usage promises those who embrace it. Another reason we should remind ourselves often: *When all else fails, try English.*

Image

The final bonus sensible language offers sensible writers is that intangible we call *image,* or *leadership,* or *persuasion.* Whether they should or not, people judge us all our lives by the way we use our language, just as they judge us by the way we dress. More and more today, your contact with others is through writing. To influence others, you must first have valuable ideas. But that itself is not enough; the way you express those ideas will have much to do in determining whether your reader accepts them with confidence.

If your reader is someone who works for you, we are describing an aspect of *leadership.* If he or she is your manager, it is *persuasiveness.* If you are writing to a customer, this same characteristic is an important part of *selling.*

Career advancement is at stake. Not by accident are the outstanding leaders in business and industry, government, the arts—in fact, in all fields—excellent communicators. That is how important writing is to everyone's career. It is probably every person's second most important skill, regardless of what field he or she is in. It is reasonable to assume that several times in your life the ability—or inability—to write will make (or has made) a difference in the advancement of your career.

Why People Write That Way

What causes intelligent adults so often to write in that overcomplicated style we have described? What can go through their minds that would cause them to reject a style that is easy to write, easy to read, and beautiful and to choose instead one that is hard to write, hard to read, and abrasive to mind and ear? Why is this Great Windbag disease so widespread?

Honestly misguided. Four common reasons explain this unfortunate attitude. The first is quite innocent: *Most people who try deliberately to write in a complex style do so because they honestly think it's the correct way and is expected of them.* Who can blame them? They see it all around them on the job. They have also read so much that is hard to understand in textbooks, professional journals, and even, sometimes, editorial pages. Who can blame people, then, for gradually getting the idea: "This is the way I'm supposed to write."

But the second, third, and fourth reasons for unnecessarily complicated writing style are not so innocent.

Lazy thinking. The second reason is: *The writer hasn't thought out his or her ideas clearly enough.* Remember, the writing process—whether for a great novel or a business letter—consists of *creating* the ideas AND *expressing* them. Every person's writing is the result of his or her thinking, on paper. But if you accept this, you must also accept that the writing cannot possibly be any clearer than the thinking.

Unfortunately, some writer's use hard-to-understand language as a substitute for clear thinking. For anyone with a good command of vocabulary and grammar skills, it is possible, and it may be quicker, to present ideas that are only half thought out, yet in a way that sounds dazzling and profound. The reader who doesn't already know the information (and most readers don't) may be fooled into thinking it—the information—is too complex to understand, when, in fact, the complexity is in the language used to convey it. (That thought process goes something like this: "I can't understand a word of this, so it must be for geniuses only." [The alternative would be: "I can't understand a word of this, so there must be something wrong with me." Given those choices, the result is predictable.]) Always be aware when you write, because this point is so important: *You cannot express an idea in ultimate clarity until you have thought it out in ultimate clarity.* And if the reader does not understand, the writer failed in his or her goal as a communicator: to broadcast his or her message in such a way that it is received fully and accurately. Nothing less will do.

The writer is a teacher. You know something your reader does not know; that's the reason you are the writer and he or she is the reader. It is not enough to say: "Here it is if you're good enough." Your job is to do everything you can to help the reader understand.

This is not to say readers, too, shouldn't participate in the thinking process. If you write with wisdom and skill, you may open new windows in the reader's mind, for further thought, or wonder. But no reader should ever wonder: "*What does this say?*"

Satisfying the ego. The third reason for heavy writing is: *trying to impress others.* The type of person guilty of this usually is a little unsure of his or her ideas, or of what the reader may think of him or her. Rather pathetically, this person is begging through the written word: "Please, won't someone notice how intelligent I am?"

Impress others with your writing, by all means. But learn from the example of professional writers—impress with the value of *what* you write, not the scholarly sound of *how* you write it. Let the impressiveness, the dignity—the beauty of your writing come from the *ideas* you express, not the *words and sentences* with which you express them. Create valuable thoughts, then deliver them in language that holds them up, on a pedestal, for everyone to see and admire. You will do more impressing this way. You are, after all, past that point in life when you could impress people with the size of your words.

Concealing weak material. The fourth reason some writers prefer unnecessarily complex style is: *to make the material seem better than it really is.* This writer knows the ideas are weak and hopes deliberately to conceal that. He or she hopes that if the work can be made to sound so complicated no one can understand it, no one will recognize it has said very little. The snow job.

Unfortunately, writers often succeed with this kind of deception quite easily; large words and twisty, winding sentences often do conceal that the ideas are not thought out very precisely. Furthermore, most readers have profound respect for things they cannot understand. They would be embarrassed to admit they cannot understand them.

Sometimes it appears the entire world is playing a sort of literary version of "The Emperor's New Clothes." Few people can understand much of what is written, but no one will admit it.

The Penguin Joke

This truck delivering a load of penguins breaks down on the way to the zoo. The day is hot, and the driver is aware his precious cargo cannot last long without air conditioning. He runs to the street, flags down the first empty truck that passes, explains the emergency to the other driver, and they quickly transfer the little darlings to the good truck. Then he hands the other driver fifty dollars and instructs him: "Take these penguins to the zoo."

Later, his truck fixed, the first driver heads back to the garage. As he passes an amusement park, he sees penguins everywhere. Penguins on the carousel, penguins on the roller coaster, penguins standing in line for popcorn. He slams on the brakes, runs into the park and finds the other driver, shakes him by the lapels, and yells: "I told you to take them to the zoo! I gave you fifty dollars and said, 'Take these penguins to the zoo!' "

And the other guy says: "I did. And we had money left over, so I brought 'em here."

Moral: No matter how clear you try to be, someone will find a way to misunderstand.

(And if you don't try, everyone will.)

(Also see: The Hippopotamus Joke, page 126.)

"The source of bad writing is the desire to be something more than a person of sense—the straining to be thought a genius. If people would only say what they have to say in plain terms, how much more eloquent they would be."

—Samuel Taylor Coleridge

CHAPTER 2

SIX PRINCIPLES OF CLEAR WRITING

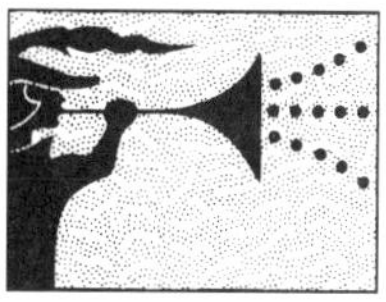

> These principles have guided authors through the centuries for writing of all kinds (except poetry). They would be equally appropriate whether you were to write a newspaper article or a great novel.

Many writing authorities begin with: *Know your reader.* This advice has to do more, however, with helping you decide WHAT you should write than HOW you should write it. Think clearly, *before* you begin the language skills part of the job, what purpose this writing should serve—what goal you want it to achieve after it is read—what effect you want it to have, and what you need to say in order to achieve that effect. Here, more than in the words and sentences part of writing, you are most likely to determine how well the writing will succeed, because no amount of good writing can win the day if the reader doesn't accept WHAT you are saying. No books or form letters can tell you what to say in any given situation. (We can, however, advise you what *not* to say: Resist telling things in great detail just to show how well informed you are on your subject.)

Help yourself by trying to picture the reader's viewpoint. You may not *agree* with that viewpoint, but if you understand the obstacles you need to overcome, you will surely be better able to overcome them.

Realistically, however, and unfortunately, writers can't always know their reader or his or her viewpoints. Still, there are important things we know about readers in general—and the reading PROCESS—that can guide us in using language to write (*encode* information) in ways that can best help those who read (*decode* it).

The six principles of clear writing are:

- Prefer clear, familiar words.
- Keep most sentences short and simple.
- Prefer active voice verbs; avoid passives.
- Refer to people in your writing.
- Use conversational style as a guide.
- Revise, revise, . . . and revise again.

In this chapter we will examine Principles 1 and 2 in detail. The other four will be discussed in Chapter 3.

PRINCIPLE 1:
Prefer Clear, Familiar Words

Have you ever stopped to think about the purpose of vocabulary? Our objectives in choosing words should be *clarity* and *precision.*

There can be no question that, in English, small words are usually the clearest and easiest to understand. This is easy to prove statistically. (For broader but quicker proof, just glance through any dictionary.) When we say writers should prefer clear, familiar words, this does *not* mean avoid using large words. Rather, avoid using an uncommon word if you can say exactly the same thing with a common one. When you use words harder to understand than necessary, you are increasing the communications line resistance between sender and receiver. Thoughtful writers will not do anything, knowingly, to increase that line resistance unnecessarily.

Therefore, do not use *facilitate* when you could say *help.* Do not use *utilize* when you could say *use,* or *endeavor* when you could say *try,* or *sufficient* when you could say *enough.*

Do not use a word like *subsequently* when you could say . . . well, as a matter of fact, what would you say instead?

Subsequently provides an example of the way large words can make a statement imprecise and create misunderstanding. When asked what it means, people are likely to give one of three responses: *next, later,* or *therefore.* Notice, however, that those meanings are different. As a matter of fact, *subsequently* can mean *next* or *later.* (But even these have different meanings.) And many writers mistakenly use it to mean *therefore,* and many readers read it that way. (The correct word would be *consequently.*) Of course, the writer knows which of those meanings he or she intends, but the reader has no way of knowing. Imprecision is introduced through a word larger than necessary.

Another such word is *parameters*—a favorite of engineers and scientists. Even dictionaries disagree what it means, and most people who use it intend it to mean *limits*—a strange misuse, probably derived from the word *perimeters.*

Or, consider the word *paradigms*—a favorite of educators. All of us could live a full life and never need this word. Worse: *paradigmatically.*

Or consider *indicated*—another favorite in business and academic writing. Does the writer mean *proved* or *suggested?* The reader can't tell. Remember, readers are paper readers, not mind readers.

Your attitude toward choice of words is a major factor in determining how clear your writing will be. Granted, *sufficient* is not much harder to read than *enough.* But it is an unnecessary overload, no matter how slight. If your attitude is to choose words harder than needed, you may do so a few times every sentence—perhaps 30 or 40 times on a page. The collective overload to the reader is devastating, as in this short example:

Solicit the employee's assistance in achieving resolution of the problem.

That means (see next page):

Ask the employee's help in solving the problem.

Imagine the burden of reading sentence after sentence, paragraph after paragraph, written in the needlessly heavy style of the first example (previous page). Readers would have little hope of receiving much information. Readers would collapse into whimpering heaps of nerves.

Small words are usually more specific. Many people are surprised to learn that *large* words, usually held in such high esteem, are often less precise. Winston Churchill called the needless use of large, difficult words *terminological inexactitude.* Does *vegetation* bring to the computer screen of the reader's mind the image of *rose bushes* or *trees*? Does *undesirable vegetation* mean *weeds*? Or does the writer intend it to mean (or might a reader think it means) *calla lilies growing where you want tomatoes*? Does *emotional reaction* mean *smiling* or *punching someone*? Is a *utensil* a *small fork* or a *frying pan*? (Similar examples can be seen often in this book.) It's hard to be vague in small words.

Remember, the writer's goal is to be precise and clear—at the receiving end.

Certainly we need the larger, less specific words when we want to make broad and general statements. (If you are writing about all items in a kitchen used for eating, cooking, or serving, *utensils* is the word.) But when our goal is to be specific, the words we turn to are usually small; if you write *the utensil,* the reader might not see the one you intended. That's how English works.

The exception: Professional terms, or Jargon. When new concepts come into our culture and require new words, more often than not these end up large words. (The reason: Languages run out of small words, and so we create new words by combining existing ones and adding Greek or Latin prefixes and suffixes—*automobile, television, computerized, refrigeration.*) In many cases words are created in that manner for specialized fields—words like *multisensory, demographics, recidivism.* Words such as these serve as a highly specialized form of shorthand for specialized professions. Readers in those professions understand them, and writers would need far more words to express those same concepts in commonly known words. A chemist, for example, needs words like *polymerization.* An engineer needs *magnetohydrodynamics;* don't bother searching for a smaller synonym. An accountant needs words like *liquidation, depreciable, profitability.*

But words like these, often called *jargon,* carry with them an important disadvantage. They are a private language—shop talk; they exclude outsiders, and the thoughtful engineer, economist, or other specialist does not use them outside the shop, when writing or speaking to general audiences.

Even such specialized terms are not always necessary, however; sometimes smaller synonyms *are* available. *Oviposition* is a scientific term for *laying eggs*—nothing more, nothing less. Here, the jargon complicates and excludes most people needlessly; it brings the disadvantage without the advantage. Likewise, an *epistaxis* is a *nosebleed,* and that's what doctors should call it; and *prenatal* is Latin for *before birth.* What's wrong with English?

Human nature, it seems, tempts people of all kinds to create special language that sets them apart from others. Did children speak *pig latin* in your childhood? *"Ids-kay at-thay ould-cay eak-spay ike-lay is-thay ere-way ecial-spay."* Everywhere, it seems, there reside people who enjoy using language to announce: "My thoughts are so special that ordinary mortals could not possibly understand them."

Develop a large vocabulary, by all means. But use it graciously; do not show off with it. Have the large words available when you need them, but you should not need most of them very often.

Remember, even though you may know the large words, your reader may not. And remember, your job is not just to broadcast but *to be received,* and you, the broadcaster, must do whatever is necessary to be received *accurately.* Anything less would be intellectually snobbish and unrealistic.

Small words add beauty. Another misguided argument is that *beauty* in writing comes from large words. No, no. The larger words may sometimes offer you the opportunity to say something complicated that could not be expressed in small ones, but certainly you could not argue that they add beauty. As a matter of fact, the large words are usually the ones that *take away* the beauty from language.

In words, the factors that contribute most to beauty are imagery and rhythm. Surely imagery is greater in small words: *joy in the eyes of a child . . . the smell of fresh cut grass. . . .*

Examine how William Maxwell, a respected American author whose life spans more than half of the 20th century, creates images—the way most good storytellers do: with small, vivid words. In this scene from his short story, *"The Fisherman Who Had Nobody to Go Out in His Boat with Him,"* we can almost see and hear the climax unfolding, as though we were there. We can certainly *feel* it:

> One evening, the fisherman didn't come home at the usual time. His wife could not hear the wind or the shutters banging, but when the wind blew puffs of smoke down the chimney, she knew that a storm had come up. She put on her cloak, and wrapped a heavy scarf around her head, and started for the strand, to see if the boats were drawn up there. Instead, she found the other women waiting with their faces all stamped with the same frightened look. Usually the seabirds circled above the beach, waiting for the fishing boats to come in and the fishermen to cut open their fish and throw them the guts, but this evening there were no gulls or cormorants. The air was empty. The wind had blown them all inland, just as, by a freak, it had blown the boats all together, out on the water, so close that it took great skill to keep them from knocking against each other and capsizing in the dark. The fishermen called back and forth for a time, and then they fell silent. The wind had grown higher and higher, and the words were blown right out of their mouths, and they could not even hear themselves what they were saying. The wind was so high and the sound so loud that it was like a silence, and out of this silence, suddenly, came the sound of singing. Being poor ignorant fishermen, they did the first thing that occurred to them—they fell on their knees and prayed. The singing went on and on, in a voice that none of them had ever heard, and so powerful and rich and deep it seemed to come from the same place that the storm came from. A flash of lightning revealed that it was not an angel, as they thought, but the fisherman who was married to the deaf-mute. He was standing in his boat, with his head bared, singing, and in their minds this was no stranger or less miraculous than an angel would have been. They crossed themselves and went on praying, and the fisherman went on singing, and in a little while the waves began to grow smaller and the wind to abate, and the storm, which should have taken days to blow itself out, suddenly turned into

Should You Spell Numbers?

Most style manuals agree with this simple rule: Spell out one-digit numbers (one through nine) and use numerals for any number having two or more digits (ten or higher).

There are some exceptions, but they are logical and simple. Use numerals for all numbers in dates and street addresses, and for numbering consecutive items (such as paragraphs), no matter how high or low.

Also, use numerals for *all* numbers in a sentence that contains both kinds (209 applicants for 5 jobs). The idea here is to be consistent within any sentence, to avoid confusing readers.

an intense calm. As suddenly as it had begun, the singing stopped. The boats drew apart as in one boat after another the men took up their oars again, and in a silvery brightness, all in a cluster, the fishing fleet came safely in to shore.

All the Days and Nights
William Maxwell (Alfred A. Knopf, publisher)

How wondrous, that tiny black lines and curlicues on a white sheet can wake such feelings. Of the 443 words, only 19 (4 percent) contain more than 2 syllables. Of those, six are the word *fisherman.* Only one word (*miraculous*) is larger.

Rhythm, too, is far easier to control with small words. Note how Edgar Allan Poe used small words to build a rhythmic beat that creates (deliberately) a distant, almost monotonous tone, reminiscent of a tom-tom beat:

Once upon a midnight dreary, while I pondered, weak and weary, over many a quaint and curious volume of forgotten lore. . . .

The Raven
Edgar Allan Poe (Doubleday, publisher)

That rhythmic pattern is called *trochaic* (each measure, or foot, is one accented syllable followed by one or more unaccented) *tetrameter* (four measures to a line). You may recognize it as the same rhythm Walt Disney used a century later in a popular movie and song:

Supercalafragilisticexpialadocious.

Mary Poppins
Walt Disney Studios

The greatest writer of all, William Shakespeare, for centuries has enthralled readers with the power and wisdom of his plays, and charmed us by composing them with long passages of formal poetic rhythm. The words in the famous passage below are the common words used in everyday life at the time he wrote. With the exception of *thou,* they are still the common ones used everyday today.

But soft! What light from yonder window breaks?*
It is the east, and Juliet is the sun.
Arise, fair sun, and kill the envious moon,
Who is already sick and pale with grief
That thou, her maid, are far more fair than she.

Romeo and Juliet
William Shakespeare

That rhythm is called *iambic* (each measure is one unaccented beat followed by one accented) *pentameter* (five measures to a line).

*We have trouble, though, with the verb at the end of the sentence in line one. The late Middle English of Shakespeare's time still carried many of the Old English traits of its teutonic (Germanic) ancestry.

SOME COMMONLY USED WORDS THAT ARE HARDER THAN NECESSARY, AND SIMPLER SUBSTITUTES

Do Not Use	*When You Could Say:*	*Do Not Use*	*When You Could Say:*
accordingly	therefore; so	indebtedness	debt
aforementioned	these	indicate	show
applicable	apply to	in order to	to
assistance	aid; help	in the event that	if
attributable	due	in the near future	soon
by means of	by	prior to	before
compensate	pay	provided that	if
consequently	so	purchase	buy
considerable	much	terminate	end
correspondence	letter	transmit	send
facilitate	help; ease	utilize	use
foregoing	this; these	visualize	see
furthermore	also	whether or not	whether
inasmuch as	because	with regard to	about

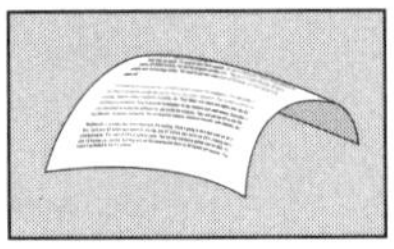

PRINCIPLE 2: Keep Most Sentences Short and Simple

Examining and learning from the styles of successful authors is one of the best ways to improve one's own style, and in the writing of most respected authors, sentences usually average between 15 and 20 words in length. You, too, should try to divide your thoughts into sentences that give readers information in clusters of reasonable size. Most students average considerably fewer than 15 words per sentence. Examine closely, and if you are in that under-15 range, look for opportunities to smooth the information flow by combining some of those very short sentences. Your readers will be grateful. Conversely, most business men and women average in the mid- or upper 20's and should look for opportunities to divide some very long ones. (This paragraph [including these two sentences] contains 152 words divided into 8 sentences. The longest is 38 words, the shortest is 5, and the average is 19 words per sentence.)

Information clusters of reasonable size. Remember, we say your sentences should *average* between 15 and 20 words in length. Mix them up. The shortest possible sentence in the English language is two words: subject and verb. There is no maximum. But caution. Again, mix them up. Do not settle into a style in which all your sentences are of medium length; the result would be a monotonous style.

Ideas should unfold in word clusters the reader can follow from beginning to end. A sentence can run quite long and still be readable. The trouble is, most people cannot write extremely long sentences very well; doing so requires exceptional grammar skills and a keen sensitivity for balancing the emphasis of major and subordinate ideas. Most people risk grammatical errors, or buried ideas, at about 30 or 35 words, and as the sentence gets longer, it becomes more likely that they will make a grammatical mistake, or that important information will go unnoticed.

Long sentences are hard to read. Like unnecessarily hard words, they increase the communications line resistance between writer and reader. Even if the writer can write long sentences and keep the grammar correct, those sentences are likely to do a poor job of transmitting the ideas. The reader may get tangled, unable to follow each idea from beginning to end. Of course, those twisty, winding sentences will almost always look clear to the writer. But always remind yourself: You, the writer, have one major advantage your reader will never have: *You know what you are trying to say.* You are not relying on those black marks on the page to find out.

One major idea to a sentence. Long sentences often contain two or more important ideas, and that is a violation of the *second half* of Principle 2: Keep Most Sentences Short AND SIMPLE. By *simple,* we mean most sentences should be devoted to only one major idea. Let the size and shape of that idea determine the size and shape of the sentence. And if you do, you are likely to end up with a rich variety of sentence lengths, averaging between 15 and 20 words per sentence.

When writers put two major ideas into one sentence, as is likely in long sentences, they risk grammatical errors. Examine this sentence:

Hon. H. H. St. Jacques
Commissioner
U.S. Interstate Commerce Commission
Washington, D.C. 20019

Dear Commissioner,

Thank you for your letter of December 18. As you requested, we are enclosing a copy of the Ex Parte 813 proposal. This is the examiner's final recommendation, quite different from your earlier study, which badly upset our client.

We do not agree with the Commission on this interpretation and plan to introduce new tariff. . . .

That is not a very long sentence—just 17 words. But it violates the second half of Principle 2, keeping major ideas in separate sentences. Of course, the flaw is obvious: Did the recommendation or the study upset the client? If you are to figure out which one, you must do so through rules of grammar or punctuation. (Realistically, however, a reader isn't likely to work that hard. In fact, a reader isn't likely even to notice that two different meanings are possible in a sentence such as that one. He or she is more likely to react subconsciously, thinking either the department's recommendation or the earlier study upset the client, unaware the statement could be read either way.)

If, as you read the passage above, you thought *the study* upset the client, you were probably reacting subconsciously to a rule of grammar you learned in 8th or 9th grade—*the rule of pronoun antecedents.* This rule tells us a pronoun will

Infamous Quotation No. 1

In 1977 President Jimmy Carter issued an order requiring all federal regulations in plain English. The implications were awesome, and there were strong reactions (mostly negative) throughout the government.

In June 1978 at the Brookings Institution, a group of legal scholars, writing experts, and government executives met to discuss the implications of the President's order. A dean of the Columbia University School of Law said, "I'm not sure I'm comfortable with the idea of legal writing in plain English. The whole thing seems sort of anti-intellectual to me."

That attitude still prevails today in the legal profession.

Ronald Reagan rescinded the Carter order, and no president has touched the subject since.

(Also see: On Legal Writing, page 75.) (Also see: Infamous Quotation No. 2, page 122.)

try to stand for the last noun before it. The pronoun is *which.* And the last noun that appears before it? *Study.* Therefore, grammar tells us *the study* upset the client.

But if you thought *the department's recommendation* upset the client, you have grammar on your side too—*the rule of nonrestrictive clauses and phrases.* This one tells us we can lift out the part between the commas and read the sentence without it. Then the sentence reads: *"This is the examiner's final recommendation, which badly upset our client."*

So, grammar tells us either meaning can be correct. Your response as a reader of that sentence, then, would depend on which rule of grammar you happen to react to subconsciously.

The writer created that blind spot because he or she tried to put two major ideas into one grammatical structure, and they would not quite fit. This is a common mistake. The longer the sentence, the more likely you will send some grammatical error to your readers.

Short sentences are hard-hitting. The shorter one is, the harder it hits, and for that reason skilled writers often build their most important ideas into sentences of very few words. Don't do this very often, however.

Short sentences are easier to write. Have you ever found yourself stuck while writing—knowing what you want to say but unable to say it? Not stuck getting started; that is an organizing problem, and we will examine this in Part 2. Rather, stuck in the middle of the writing. Then ask yourself, "Where am I stuck?" At precisely what point in the writing?

Notice carefully the next time this happens. You will probably find you are stuck in the middle of a sentence. Writers can always start one; finishing some of them, however, may give us fits. When you are stuck, the grammatical structure is probably wrong for the ideas. Probably you have too many ideas in that sentence, and the grammar will not fit them all—or is pushing you in a direction you do not wish to go.

How do you get unstuck in such a situation? Inexperienced writers stagger desperately to the next period to get out of that mess. (We can tell because they leave the mess behind for the reader to clean up.) When you are stuck in the middle of a sentence, do not stagger on. Rather, retreat to the last period and start again. Separate that long sentence into two, three, or four short ones. You should soon be unstuck, able to say what you want with little trouble.

Sentence sense should save you time. Just by dividing ideas into sentences easily *and naturally,* you can probably write considerably faster than you do. It is those long, awkward sentences that slow you down so much.

Instant help: the meat cleaver technique. This is another working tool of professional writers. Often you can help a long sentence greatly by simply chopping it into two shorter ones.

Help is needed when the sentence contains two or more major ideas, one after the other, and the reader's brain is forced to drag an increasingly heavy load as it plods toward, hoping for, the next period. Chop the long sentence neatly in two. Sometimes doing so is as easy as changing a comma to a period and beginning the second half with a capital letter. Other times it may be necessary to cauterize the wound—change a few words to restore proper grammar after the chop.

You need not always divide separate ideas into separate statements. If the two major ideas are short, they will not overburden the reader as one sentence. But if it gets very long, more than 25 or 30 words, the sentence may overburden the reader, and over 35 words it almost certainly will. Consider chopping it in two. This is probably the easiest and most immediate way of improving your writing—and saving time.

Here you see an example of the *meat cleaver technique* and how it makes the writing clearer. First, the original:

The Shore Engineering District has requested the installation of a CD-ROM terminal at 18419 River Road, where the satellite downlinks will be located, for the purpose of providing SED designers access to the new authoring software.

Here is the logical breaking point:

The Shore Engineering District has requested the installation of a CD-ROM terminal at 18419 River Road, where the satellite downlinks will be loaded, • for the purpose of providing SED designers access to the new authoring software.

Here is what the *meat cleaver technique* can do. Notice that in this example it was necessary to do a little rewording at the chop:

The Shore Engineering District has requested the installation of a CD-ROM terminal at 18419 River Road, where the satellite downlinks will be located. Its purpose will be to provide SED designers access to the new authoring software.

Long sentences may bury ideas. Limiting sentences to one major idea does not mean ruling out subordinate clauses. Rather, use subordinate clauses for subordinate ideas. Subordinate means *less important.* It's unwise to put two *major* ideas in the same sentence; even if you can keep the grammar straight, you end up with buried ideas. They are likely to compete for emphasis, for the reader's attention, and when this happens one wins and the other loses. Or they share equally, and neither idea gets the full attention it deserves.

Here is an example of a major idea buried as a subordinate clause. The buried part is between the first and last commas:

The Society's loss of its IRS nonprofit status, which, we were informed by Jennie Frisina, director of the Office of Special Events, was the direct result of the director's actions against the wishes of the board of trustees, prevented the singers from performing in the children's program.

Here is the same thing rewritten as two sentences, with that buried idea getting full emphasis:

The Society's loss of its IRS nonprofit status prevented the singers from performing in the children's program. We were informed by Jennie Frisina, Director of the Office of Special Events, that the loss was the direct result of the director's actions against the wishes of the board of trustees.

THE PERIOD IS THE NOBLEST PUNCTUATION MARK OF THEM ALL—and the one that can solve the most problems. Generally, you can safely assume: The more you concentrate on using periods correctly, the better the writing will be.

But caution: Although an occasional short sentence, even as short as a few words, can be remarkably effective, *too many* short sentences make the writing sound childish. Worse, they create problems for readers by causing all ideas to sound equally important (because they don't allow the use of many subordinate [less important] phrases or clauses):

> The new software works perfectly. I learned how to use it by attending the Bentleyville seminar. This was included in the purchase price. We should now be able to send out food distribution reports before noon every Tuesday. That has been our experience so far. The review committee has been requesting we do this. The reports are shorter than in the past. Color graphics make the usage and cost data easier to read. We no longer need to transfer database information. The first week, some of the continuous report forms jammed in the feeder. The Bentleyville group corrected this malfunction. It had nothing to do with the software.
>
> *(108 words, 12 sentences, averaging 9 words per sentence. Not very inspiring, and extremely hard to follow. Longest sentence 15 words, shortest 5.)*

Readers can't receive information that way very long. Did you want to scream as you read it?

Try combining some short sentences if the average is under 15 words per sentence. In doing this you will not be just manipulating numbers; you will be changing the grammatical (and logical) relationships between ideas, to make them easier to follow. In the things we write about, not all ideas are equally important; some need more—or less—attention than others, and the writer's skill in dividing ideas into sentences determines how much attention each idea gets. We can give one idea a loud voice and another a soft one; that is why languages give us subordinate phrases and clauses. Or, when we feel two very short ideas are equally important, we can give them equal emphasis by placing one after the other in the same sentence, combining them with a connective (conjunction) such as *and* or *but.* Remember, readers cannot *feel* the relationships between ideas the way you, the writer, can. Readers are paper readers, not mind readers. They need to *see* those relationships, and you must help them do so:

> The new software works perfectly, and I learned to use it by attending the Bentleyville seminar included in the purchase price. Based on our experience so far, we should now be able to send out food distribution reports by noon every Tuesday, as the review committee has been requesting. The new reports are shorter, and the color graphics make the usage and cost data easier to read. Another advantage is that we no longer need to transfer database information. The first week, some of the continuous report forms jammed in the feeder, but the Bentleyville support group has corrected this malfunction. It had nothing to do with the software.
>
> *(109 words, 6 sentences, averaging a very respectable 18.2 words per sentence. Longest sentence, 28 words; shortest, 8. The division of ideas into sentences of appropriate length makes writing and reading easier; the variety of sentence lengths makes both more interesting.)*

DEVIL'S ADVOCATE: Going back to choice of words, I understand what you're saying, but I'm a little puzzled. Why should a person enlarge his or her vocabulary if not to use some of those esoteric and recondite words?

GURU: Okay. I know what *"esoteric"* and *"recondite"* mean, and I'll try to ignore that you used them. Of course we should all continue enlarging our vocabularies. As long as writers continue to use little-known words, and as long as libraries contain books by those writers, you should keep developing your vocabulary as a *reader.* Otherwise you'll miss information you might want to know.

DEVIL'S ADVOCATE: From poor writers!

GURU: No, from writers who wrote in a time when attitudes on language differed from ours today. Or, even if writers today are . . . let's say . . . misguided on language usage, they might still be saying things you want or need to know. Be tolerant. Tolerance is good for your well being. And useful information is useful even if you have to work harder than necessary for it. In fact, that's the whole trouble. Poor writing usually deprives us of useful knowledge, not junk.

DEVIL'S ADVOCATE: I can write long sentences and keep the grammar correct. Why shouldn't I?

GURU: Go ahead. But only if you're willing to say, "It's okay if my readers don't get my message; that's their problem; I did my job." But did you? Grammatically correct doesn't mean clear. Two things tend to create confusion when your little black marks on the page combine too many ideas into too few sentences: First, modifiers may get separated from the words they modify and latch onto a word you didn't intend, changing your meaning; and second, from your readers' point of view, punctuation may become so complex that those little curlicues down there don't give readers strong enough signals to turn the directions you want them to go. These are unnecessary barriers, little confusion-makers. Will your readers take the trouble to overcome them? Will readers even be *aware* if they misinterpret an important point?

DEVIL'S ADVOCATE: Don't short sentences sound choppy: "*Run, Spot, run. See Spot run*"? Is this the image writers want to send?

GURU: But that was three words per sentence. You never listen. We said average between 15 and 20. Let the size and shape of the idea determine the size and shape of the sentence, and if you do, there will be many longer ones to balance any very short ones. You're right, however; short sentences can produce choppy passages, and skillful writers are constantly snooping around for choppiness and know how to prevent it. That's why *connectives* are so useful; they bridge the logic gap between the end of the last idea and the beginning of the next one.

DEVIL'S ADVOCATE: This new attitude about short sentences is intriguing—the concept that impact is inversely proportional to length.

GURU: Don't do this to me. Surely you mean: the shorter a sentence is, the harder it hits. Listen, go back and reread Chapter 2, and don't return until you have a better attitude about the purpose of words.

DEVIL'S ADVOCATE: Well, . . .

GURU: Just do it. Trust me; I'm your friend.

DEVIL'S ADVOCATE: Okay, but look. You're advocating a way of writing that's pretty new and different for most people. In real life, supposing the *reader*—who may be my manager, or the instructor in a course I'm taking—believes the opposite about words and sentences and *wants* the writing to sound scholarly? You said that's a common misconception.

GURU: Yes, and you raise a thoughtful point. Your manager or instructor may indeed believe that; lots of very capable and nice people do. So, in the real world, if he or she insists, you may be forced to use larger words than necessary, or complex sentences, or both. But always remember—and this is important: Writing in a particular style, in a particular situation, for a particular reason, is far different from writing that way all the time because you believe it's the only correct way.

DEVIL'S ADVOCATE: If every writer uses easy words and sentences, won't we all sound alike? Wouldn't that sameness destroy style?

GURU: Au contraire, mes amis. Quite the contrary, my friends. It's the preconceived notion that language needs to be complicated that destroys individual style. All writers who practice that style sound like all the others, and they all sound like a government report on the price of cabbages. Shedding this notion grants you the freedom to sound like yourself.

On the other hand, you may in a particular situation *want* to sound colorless and hopelessly complicated. The point is, at all times you should want—and know how—to control this.

International Writing Institute, Inc.
Hanna Building • 1422 Euclid Avenue • Cleveland, OH 44115-1993
Phone: 216-696-8100 • Fax: 216-696-8101

12 words Good writing almost always averages between 15 and 20 words per sen-
23 tence. Do not write all sentences within these limits, however, because
3 doing so would make your style so dull it would bore your reader. Mix them
37 up. Although most people probably are not aware of it, readers feel comfortable with the changing pace we experience when the sentences are
occasionally as short as 3 or 4 words or as long as 30 or 35.

9 There are reasons your favorite authors are your favorites. Skilled writers do
27 many things with language to create exactly the mood they want, and one of
the most effective of these is control of sentence length.

12 Short sentences give emphasis; the shorter one is, the harder it hits. They
also create the feeling of action. This is because shorter sentences mean
7 more sentences and therefore more verbs. Verbs are the action words, and
12 so skilled writers deliberately use short sentences to create the tense, fast-
23 moving mood appropriate for action passages.

Long sentences, on the other hand, are generally useful for the slower pace
necessary in descriptive passages, as important for proper balance as the
25 action. They meander along, like peaceful stretches of a river, at the relaxed
35 speed best suited for detailed viewing, slowly, deliberately unfolding information about the people, places, and things that provide the background for
the actions. Although an important part of most writing, these passages tend
25 to subordinate the ideas they contain and therefore are generally ineffective
for presenting major ideas.

19 It is the combination of these two techniques that causes readers to say, "I
couldn't put the book down."
269

The shortest sentence in this passage is 3 words, and the longest is 37. The average is a very readable 19 words per sentence.

CHAPTERS 1 AND 2

REVIEW

How alert were you? All of these important questions were discussed in the chapter you just read. You should be able to answer them all. If you cannot, it's in your interest to look them up.

Please list the three major benefits of good writing, which are also the objectives of the advice in this book.

Clarity
Speed
Image

What are the four most common reasons intelligent adults write in an unnecessarily complicated style?

Honesty - Misguided
Lazy Thinking
Satisfying the Ego.
Concealing weak material

What two separate factors must every writer always deal with when writing?

Ability to choose words and
build them into sentences

What three major advantages do small words have over large ones?

Clear and easiest to understand
More specific
Add beauty

What are the disadvantages of long sentences? (Four were mentioned in the text; you may be able to add others.)

Poor job in transmitting the ideal.
Usually contain two or more major ideas.
Risk grammatical errors
Take too much time to write, slow you down -
Bury ideals.

What should be the average number of words per sentence? 15 - 20 words

It is desirable for ***all*** *sentences to be that length. True or false?* False

PRACTICE

Small words add clarity and beauty.

CHAPTERS 1 AND 2

EXERCISES

Exercise 1.

Opposite each word or group of words below, write a word that better says the same thing. (For some, you may need a few words):

	Your Word:	*Recommended:*
Detrimental	un real, Shocking	
Simultaneously	contineously	
Sufficient	Important	
Consequently	resalt	
Possesses	have	
Capability	able	
Numerous	many	
Punctual	on time	
Molecular		
Endeavor	bear	
Verification	proof	
Concur		
Deferral		
Accelerate	Pick up, increase	
In close proximity	Near by	
Take cognizance of	recognize	
At the present time	Now, at this time	
In the event that	When	
Due to the fact that	because	
Maximum quantity	More than, Most	
Minimum quantity	Less than, Fewer	
Termination	Fired	
Excessive	More than	

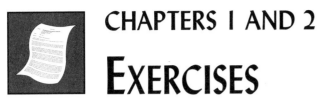

PRACTICE

Small words require clear thinking.

Exercise 2.

Large words often make writing unclear. By obscuring ideas, they sometimes fail to communicate, as in this example. Try saying the exact same thing in simpler words:

> *Our inability to approve your application for credit is based on insufficient down payment. We are concerned with the potential inability to meet repayment obligations as scheduled, due to inadequate income.*

Your Rewrite

Thank you for your application For Credit, however, our discision of denial was based on insufficient income to meet repayment obligations.

Recommended

Exercise 3.

Large words may make your writing sound cold, robbing it of charm. Try rewriting this passage with smaller words to make it not only clearer but in a more relaxed, warmer tone:

> *Mr. McWayte addressed the Rock 'n' Roll Division's May staff meeting. Attendees were duly impressed with the multitudinous tasks involved in the accumulation of relevant, pertinent recording data and the methodology by which these tasks are implemented by the MCS staff.*

PRACTICE

Small words help you sound courteous.

Your Rewrite

The Rock 'n' Roll Division May Staff Meeting was presented by Mr. McWayte. Our guest, the MCS Staff impressed all attendees with an overview of the many tasks for recording accumulated pertinent data.

Recommended

PRACTICE

Too many short sentences make you sound childish.

Exercise 4.

The words in this passage are reasonable for the message, but the tone is choppy and childish. Try to improve it by combining six very short sentences into fewer longer ones, just by changing punctuation and rewording slightly where you do:

> *We like this company's work. The wooden forms needed for pouring concrete are always accurate. And delivery is usually on time. They have been late only once since we started using them. That was during the railroad strike last year. Unfortunately, their price for this job is too high.*

Your Rewrite

We like this company because they usualley deliver on time & wooden forms are always accurate for pouring of the concrete. Since we started using them, they have been late only once during the railroad strike last year. Unforturately, their price for the job is too high.

Recommended

PRACTICE

Short sentences are clear, hard-hitting.

r and its ideas stronger by chopping it into
leaver technique):

astball and has a changeup and good
ince he was named rookie of the year
-out single to Rod Brewer in the first
ers, throwing ten straight balls at one

Your Rewrite

fast ball suffered his worst detat
the year two seasons ago. He has
. Throwing ten straight balls at
singe to Rod Brewer in the first
f batters.

Recommended

PRACTICE

Short sentences are easier to write.

Exercise 6.

This one requires more than just chopping. You will have to simplify some words as well:

> *This kind of action should be formal and direct, involving thorough analysis of all pertinent factors and presentation of a wide range of specific alternatives such that the GW supervisor merely has to choose from an array of facts which by their mere presence instills confidence and assurance that GW employees are getting the best benefits program that is available.*

(By the way, did you notice the grammatical error? Errors of this kind become more likely as the sentence gets longer.)

Your Rewrite

Recommended

PRACTICE

Shorter sentences: the key to clear legal writing.

Exercise 7. (optional)

Even financial or legal statements, which so often baffle readers, can be thoroughly readable. The passage below can be improved greatly just by breaking two monstrously long sentences into several shorter ones. But you can improve it still further by using easier words and trimming wasted words. You don't have to be a lawyer or a financial expert to do this:

> *The attached Statement of Consolidated Income for the six months ended June 30, 1995 and June 30, 1994 for the Standard Chair Company (a Michigan corporation) and consolidated subsidiary companies has been prepared in accordance with accepted accounting principles from the books of the companies.*
>
> *Pursuant to Section 5.1 of the Note Agreement dated June 15, 1995 providing for the issuance and sale by the Standard Chair Company of $50,000,000 aggregate principal amount of 9.55% notes due July 15, 2015, the undersigned, an authorized officer, does hereby certify that, to the best of my knowledge, the Standard Chair Company has performed and observed all of, and is not at the date hereof in default in the performance or observance of any of the terms, provisions, or conditions of said Note Agreement and that there exists no Event of Default, as defined by Section 9.1 of same.*

Your Rewrite

(Continued on next page)

EXERCISE 7 Your rewrite (continued):

Recommended

Notes

"The first human being who hurled a curse instead of a weapon against his adversary was the founder of civilization."

—SIGMUND FREUD

CHAPTER 3

Six Principles of Clear Writing (*continued*)

Approach each writing task with the attitude: It is possible to express even your most difficult ideas clearly and simply, *with no sacrifice of accuracy.* Once you begin feeling comfortable about plain English, you may also feel a new kind of satisfaction as artistry creeps into your writing, and as a new kind of dignity becomes evident—the dignity that is part of, and comes from, your message.

Chapter 2 discussed the two most important principles of clarity: familiar words and easy sentences. Here, now, are the other four of the six principles of clear writing:

- Prefer active voice verbs; avoid passives.
- Refer to people in your writing.
- Use conversational style as a guide.
- Revise, revise, . . . and revise again.

PRINCIPLE 3: Prefer Active Voice Verbs; Avoid Passives

Recall the school year when you were learning the basics of sentence structure, and your English teacher probably began with some sentence like, "*The dog buried the bone.*" You were introduced then to those basic terms—subject, transitive verb, direct object. *(Dog–buried–bone.)*

That sentence structure is the backbone of the English language. It is in the ACTIVE voice. The same thing in the passive voice would be: "*The bone was buried by the dog.*"

An invitation to misunderstanding: A business manager might write: "*Our engineering department approved the plan.*" Notice that this is the same structure as "*The dog buried the bone*": Subject, transitive verb, direct object.

(Engineering department–approved–plan.) Winston Churchill described this structure as "The Noble English Sentence."

In the passive voice, that statement would be: "*The plan was (or has been) approved by our engineering department.*" Notice that in the passive version the subject is *plan.* The verb is still *approved,* but it has picked up the auxiliary (helping verb) *was.* And the object is now *engineering department.* SUBJECT AND OBJECT HAVE TRADED PLACES.

In the active voice, which is the more natural way, the subject performs the action described by the verb (its role is active), and the object receives it. In the passive, instead of performing the action the subject *receives* the action of the verb. (The role of the subject is passive). Because it has that little helping verb (in this case "*was*"), a passive is a *complete* verb, not a transitive verb. It doesn't need an object. If you examine the grammatical structure in the passive version of the sentence above, you soon notice that the object (formerly the subject) is no longer the direct object (of a transitive verb); rather, it has become the *indirect* object of the preposition *by.* But the entire prepositional phrase, *by our engineering department,* is an unnecessary part of the grammar. It hangs there awkwardly, and writers are tempted to drop out such passages. Then our sentence reads: "*The plan was (or has been) approved.*"

Now the sentence does not tell *by whom.* And, more often than many writers realize, *by whom* is an important part of the information. The writer knows who did what but may not notice that the sentence doesn't share this information with the reader. The reader, too, may be unaware some information is missing and, in filling the gap intuitively, may assume wrongly. The writer's mind sees: "*Our engineering department approved the plans,*" but the reader's mind may see: "*The village council approved. . . .*" or, "*the Environmental Protection Agency approved. . . .*" Thoughtful writers do not give readers such choices.

These two samples show the importance of that *by whom* information:

The following procedure *is recommended:*

When the red light goes on, the instrument *should be shut* down and all settings *should be checked.* It *should be turned* on again only when it *is confirmed* that all pressures are within tolerances.

Notice how much more information the active voice conveys:

The union recommends the following procedure:

When the red light goes on, the operator should shut the instrument down and the supervisor should check all settings. The lab assistant should turn it on again only when the research manager confirms that all pressures are within tolerances.

At no time is a passive more risky than in the writing of procedures, or other written instructions. Do not write, "*The statement must be updated every three months. . . .*" The work might not get done. You are saying something must be done but not who must do it. The reader may not realize he or she is supposed to do it. Rather write, "*You must update the statement every three months . . .*"

(or whoever else). Notice the difference? The active voice is clearer and more emphatic, and therefore the instructions are more likely to be followed.

The passive is not always wrong, however. Sometimes *by whom* is obvious or not important. For example, in a research report a scientist is usually describing his or her own work. *By whom* is obvious, and if he or she were to report the various stages of that work in the active voice the subject would repeatedly be *I*. That would be awkward and inappropriate. In this case the passive would probably be better.

Or, *by whom* may be unimportant: "The tension *was broken* only when the last of the missing paintings *was recovered.*" But even when the passive does not conceal information, it risks making the writing dull. Therefore, careful writers should use it sparingly.

Compare:

Boudreau described those events in detail, and now Carrabini and Hall realized that the two young officers had fooled everyone.

. . . with:

Those events were described in detail, and it was now realized that everyone had been fooled.

Caution: *passive* and *past* are not the same. They sound somewhat alike only by accident. Do not assume that all passive voice verbs are in the past tense; they occur in all tenses. We could say, *The plans were approved. . . . The plans are being approved. . . .* or *The plans will be approved.* There you have past, present, and future tenses. But they are all passive, and all equally weak for the same reason.

Passives are easy to recognize. They all have some form of the verb *to be* (that helping verb) in front of the main verb. *"The plan **was** approved." "The statement **must be** updated." "Everyone **had been** fooled."* After you have recognized a verb is in the passive voice, turning it active is simple. Just ask yourself: By whom? The answer to that question gives you the subject you need for an active voice sentence. "*It is recommended that we make the changes,*" By whom? *The Atlanta office recommends that we make the changes.*" Or, "*I recommend that we make the changes.*" "*Mary is loved.*" By whom? John? Gregorio? Everyone who knows her? *By whom* can make a great difference to your reader.

BUT NOTE: Not all forms of the verb *to be* are passive. This may sound complicated, but it isn't. If verbs such as *was, is, are,* and *will be* stand alone, without another verb form, they themselves are complete verbs in the active voice. Like passives, these verbs don't need an object.

Smedley *was* our player of the year last year. She *is* the league's best shooting guard and *will be* a strong candidate for most valuable player if her numbers continue at this pace. (All three are active voice forms of the berb to *be*.)

In the last example, *was, is,* and *will be* are not helping verbs in front of another verb; they are the whole verb. But:

Smedley *was voted* our player of the year last year. She *is described* as the league's best shooting guard and *will be considered* a strong candidate for most valuable player if her numbers continue at this pace. (All three are passive voice verbs.)

Now compare that information with:

Female and male faculty members of the athletic department *voted* Smedley our player of the year last year. Opposing players *describe* her as the league's best shooting guard, and sports writers *will consider* her a strong candidate for most valuable player if her numbers continue at this pace.

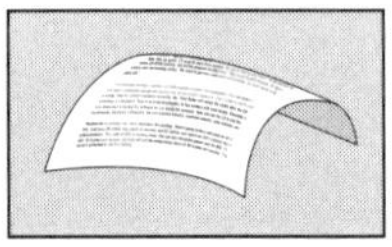

PRINCIPLE 4: Refer to People in Your Writing

A widespread superstition holds that expository writing should be impersonal whenever possible. Misguided writers have even coined a name for the style that avoids references to people: *third person.* But when we ask ourselves, "Why should we avoid references to human beings?", the whole idea doesn't seem to serve any purpose. In fact, it usually does more harm than good.

What tempts people to write in this impersonal style? Usually they don't know. The answer usually given is *"Well, it's always been done that way."* An inadequate explanation. (Note, incidentally, that *"it's always been done"* is in the passive voice [*has been done*]. The active voice version of that statement would be *"We've always done* [*have done*] *it that way."* This example illustrates an interesting point: The urge to avoid references to people often places writers in the passive voice. Conversely, writers who feel comfortable referring to people almost always operate in the active voice, whether they know it or not, because active voice verbs usually need people as subjects.)

People are often an important part of what we are writing about. Why pretend otherwise? By all means refer to them in your writing.

This advice does not mean pulling people in artificially. Rather, don't go out of your way to keep them out of your writing. Refer to people and companies by their names. Certainly you may call people *he, she,* or *they.* In fact, you may even call yourself *I.* There is absolutely no restriction against this—but there is one sensible limitation: Your English teachers probably told you, "Don't repeat *I, I, I,* over and over again." They were right. But an occasional *I* is perfectly proper—even in the most serious and dignified writing.

Some people argue that impersonal tone (without references to people) is a sign the writer was thinking objectively—that *cold logic* means "human beings prohibited." When you stop and think about it, however, why would this be? Tone can be deceptive. One can imagine a piece of writing being badly biased, yet seeming (to casual readers) to be objective because a scholarly and impersonal tone creates the *impression* of objectivity. Likewise, a warm, personal tone can be equally deceptive, creating a false impression of *agreement* while presenting information that opposes the reader's views. Language skills can give writers that kind of power—the power to deceive. There is simply no relationship between the tone of the writing and the objectivity of the writer.

But caution: Do not use *I* and *we* interchangeably; doing so would be inappropriate. Use *I* when referring to yourself and *we* when referring to yourself and someone else. When you are in doubt, *we* is probably appropriate.

Generally, referring to people will make your writing sound more courteous and pleasant. More important, the writing will be more informative and precise.

PRINCIPLE 5: Use Conversational Style as a Guide

For adults with reasonable (not necessarily outstanding) vocabulary and grammar skills, spoken language gently coaxes us toward expressing things the way they should be expressed. (The reason: In all cultures, spoken language developed long before writing appeared [about 5,000 years ago]. Language patterns, therefore,—and vocabulary—were well established before our earliest ancestors began to think about things like alphabets and writing.)

The advice, **use conversational style,** however, does not mean to write in slang or in a careless way. Writing should be more precise than conversation, because the writer has more time to choose words and build sentences carefully—and the reader has more time to be critical. He or she will usually ignore some carelessness in our talking but will not forgive that same carelessness in our writing.

In addition to the historical fact that spoken language came much earlier than writing, there are two practical reasons most people communicate more effectively in speaking. First, we have had far more practice speaking than writing; we have done it every day since approximately age two. Second, in conversation the situation itself is more likely to improve the transfer of information. Most of our speaking in our lifetimes is face to face, and so we get instant feedback—chances to correct any mistakes. With the receiver right there, we have many ways of knowing when we aren't communicating effectively—a questioning look on the other person's face, or the blunt statement, "I don't understand." Even though we may not have been aware it was happening, that instant feedback has helped us improve our speaking skills since those very early years when we were just beginning to construct language patterns in our minds.

As a result, most people have two distinct personalities when they communicate. The difference between them is so pronounced there seems almost to be a switch in the back of the head, with one position for speech, the other for writing. The purpose of Principle 5, then, is to help you to write with your switch in the speaking position. But doing so may not be easy.

Here is another important piece of advice from professional writers. When you are having trouble finding just the right way to express an idea in writing, ask yourself: "How would I say this to a loved one or a friend at dinner tonight?" Again, it may not be easy, but if you can force yourself to imagine how you would express that idea to someone in relaxed conversation, in a casual surrounding, that is likely to be a better way of writing it. Another version of the same technique: *How would your favorite TV newscaster say it?*

No doubt you can remember at some time reading something you couldn't understand, so you asked the writer, who replied: "What I mean is. . . ."—then went on to tell you in simple, precise English. You then answered, "Okay, thanks . . . ," and you probably muttered to yourself: "Why didn't you write it that way in the first place?" He or she probably should have.

Again, that warning, however. Most of us use language a bit carelessly in conversation. You must be more careful in writing than in talking to choose the right words, and to build them into grammatically correct sentences. But that should not be very challenging. You will probably have no trouble using correct grammar if you try to avoid dangerously long and complicated sentences. The true Principle 5, then, should probably read: "*Use a conversational style; well, sort of, anyhow.*"

PRINCIPLE 6: Revise, Revise, . . . and Revise Again

No letter or report, no great book, was ever written (except through the Divine hand of God) that couldn't be made better if the writer had one more chance to read and revise.

I call, at this point, upon the author's privilege to address the reader in the first person. The principles presented in this book have served me well as a writer and teacher. But applying them has not always been quick or easy. Our writing should be easy to read, but our readers may never know the difficulty—the anguish—we sometimes go through to get it that way. *Thinking* exactly what we want to say, then *saying* it with reasonable language skill, may sometimes be sublimely simple, or at other times so hard we may doubt our ability to do it in a particular passage, and when we succeed we usually know it, and the satisfaction is great. Even so, I find it unthinkable that the *first version* of any writing could not be made better. It just doesn't happen that way.

Why revise if you have already done your best? Well, let's say you have done your best *so far.* We all have blind spots, and to find and correct them we must separate ourselves from our work. Only then, *we* can see our work as our *readers* see it. The further (longer) the separation, the more weaknesses we are able to see and correct.

Blind spots are idea gaps—passages, large or small, that didn't quite say what we intended, or perhaps how we intended, but we can't see the gap. Neither, if the writing *seems* clear, can the reader. All of us have revisited something we wrote earlier and wondered: *Did I write that?*

The trouble is inherent in the nature of language and the brain. Our thoughts exist as electrical charges, not words. Writers (or speakers) convert their information to words just for the transmission, and readers (or listeners) convert them back. Picture yourself as you sit there during the writing process. We monitor our work as we write—almost as though standing over our own shoulder, looking down as a typical reader would, and constantly asking: "*How am I doing?*" The trouble comes because too often our brain answers: "*Fine.*" The trouble comes because each of us is the *least* typical reader of our own writing. *We* know what we are trying to say; *we* are not relying on those little black marks on the page to find out. No other reader can have that privilege. And so, if a passage comes close but does not say exactly what we intended, or says it a little awkwardly, we tend to see not what we wrote but what we *intended.* An idea gap exists, but the writerbrain fills in the missing information involuntarily. No readerbrain can do that; readers are paper readers, not mind readers. The reader may have trouble understanding, or dislike something we said awkwardly, or may not be aware he or she is missing anything.

Later, when we are no longer so close to that work, we *can* see our writing as a typical reader would. Then we see our gaps in logic, or our awkward phrases, and can correct them.

And that is the final part of the writing process.

DEVIL'S ADVOCATE: Suppose—this is concerning passive verbs—a person makes a mistake—let's say, in figuring the cost of a job. Wouldn't it be smarter to say, "*The cost was figured incorrectly . . .*" than "*I figured the . . .*"?

GURU: (Sigh.) Must I explain things you should have learned from your parents? Yours is not a language question; it's a judgment question. Yes, deception is one of the recognized uses of language, so the question is reasonable, and in this case the passive voice does conceal some troublesome information. But even if that's what you want to do, the more important and practical question may be: How well does it conceal it? Sooner or later, it seems, you're going to end up in the active voice, because it's likely someone will ask, "By whom?" Is this little deception cool, then?

DEVIL'S ADVOCATE: Clarify something else, please. That example at the beginning of this chapter, "*Our engineering department approved the plan . . .*" Suppose that said, "*. . . has approved the plan.*" Now there's a form of *to be* in front of the main verb, but it isn't passive.

GURU: Uh-huh. Good question. You're right; it's in the active voice, not passive, because the subject is *performing* the action. And that's the only fully accurate way of recognizing whether a verb is active or passive. *Has approved* is the verb form called *past participle,* active voice. Its subject is performing the action. It is passive when the subject is *receiving* the action.

GURU: Here's another thing about passives: The two parts of the verb *are* sometimes (as here) *separated.* "*The plan was* quickly *approved by our engineering department*"; nothing changed in the basic structure of the sentence.

DEVIL'S ADVOCATE: Is it true that once the writing is started in the active or passive voice you should stay with it—you can't switch from one to the other . . . or maybe, not until the next paragraph?

GURU: Who dreamed that one up? Of course you may. (You just used both, in

Why write, when a phone call is easier?

For four important reasons:

(1) You have more time in writing than in conversation to present your thoughts effectively.

(2) The reader can't say things you may not be prepared to discuss. (If discussion is needed, a phone call and confirming letter are best.)

(3) A letter is harder to ignore at the other end. Because it stays there, it is more likely to get attention.

(4) If your message will be forwarded to someone else, it goes in *your* carefully chosen words.

As for speed, with today's technology a fax letter can get there as fast as a phone call or electronic mail.

the perfectly natural wording of your question.) It would be impossible to write very long, sticking to all active or all passive voice. Maybe you were told you shouldn't change verb *tenses,* but that advice is also wrong and would also be impossible to follow.

DEVIL'S ADVOCATE: Referring to people in formal writing seems a little pushy. We were always told it's in poor taste . . . bad manners . . . unless you're writing a personal letter, or a novel or short story.

GURU: It's not a matter of etiquette; it's a matter of reporting accurately, and people are often (usually?) an important part of the things we write about, especially in the world after academia. Why try to pretend they don't exist? Let's take a constructive approach. Examine the word *I.* Certainly it's appropriate to refer to yourself as *I* or *me* in a report or letter; just don't do it too often: *I* noticed . . . , *I* concluded . . . , *I* believe. . . . Even here, it's not so much a question of good manners; it's a question of *accuracy,* for this reason: When people look around and observe themselves to be the center of the universe, they probably aren't observing very accurately. Maybe that's the reason they make readers uncomfortable.

DEVIL'S ADVOCATE: How about *the undersigned?*

GURU: Oh, come off it. That creates the image of a 1930's office, and you wearing a green eyeshade and sleeve garters, sitting under a bare lightbulb that hangs from a single wire. How odd that anyone would sneer at *I* but profoundly respect *the undersigned;* they mean exactly the same thing today, and, therefore, both must be equally proper or improper. Once, *the undersigned* was a respected term. It became fashionable when people of high rank had secretaries and clerks who were good at composition (and penmanship) who would write their letters for them. Everyone knew that the person who signed the letter hadn't written it; the phrase, then, became a symbol of the important and privileged person. As that happened, people of lesser rank began using the phrase—a little deception to elevate oneself in the eyes of one's reader. People would write, "*The undersigned holds you dear to his heart.*" How very odd.

DEVIL'S ADVOCATE: You're convincing me, but who will convince my boss? The Six Principles may be okay here; the trouble is they're not the way things are done in my company. My boss won't buy into this way of writing.

GURU: Don't be sure. But also, don't get fired. The thing is, managers are usually eager for better ways of doing things, but often people use the excuse: "*Oh, the boss will never allow that,*" without asking a simple question to find out.

Still, it may be true occasionally that a manager believes good writing should sound scholarly and cold. In that case, try to convince him or her of the advantages of plain English. Usually you can, if you can convince him or her of two basic points: First, that the *content* doesn't change; you're still the same person, using the same judgment, in deciding WHAT a letter should or should not contain. And second, that the new style, though maybe more relaxed, is still dignified. If the boss remains unconvinced, then of course you must write the way he or she wants. But—and I told you this before—writing in a particular style, in a particular situation, for a particular reason, is far different from writing that way regularly because you think it's the only correct way.

DEVIL'S ADVOCATE: About rewriting . . .

GURU: Let's not even discuss it, except to say: *You need to rewrite, and the more important the document, the more times you should rewrite and rewrite again.* Trust me; I'm your friend. Nor does this need diminish as we become more experienced writers. *Quod erat demonstrandum.*

DEVIL'S ADVOCATE: What?

GURU: Thus it has been demonstrated.

It's FebRUary, for goodness sake!

Let's start a national campaign to banish FebUary. This is a spoken naynay, never a written one, and those who care about it begin worrying in January that life next month will have painful moments.

We would like to think only klutzes say FebUary, but even some respected radio and television journalists have fallen to this heinous crime. Males and females seem equally guilty; nor have other demographic variances been identified.

CHAPTER 3

REVIEW

How alert were you? All of these important questions were discussed in the chapter you just read. You should be able to answer them all. If you cannot, you are urged to look them up.

When the writer uses passive voice verbs, he or she often fails to tell the reader:

What is the grammatical structure of most English language sentences?

How does a passive voice verb change this?

What do all passives have in common that makes them easy to recognize?

Briefly describe the recommended attitude toward getting people into your writing:

What is the correct usage of I *and* we?

What question should you ask yourself as an aid when having trouble expressing an idea clearly?

What advantage does speaking have over writing?

What advantage does writing have over speaking?

What warning should you keep in mind when using conversational style?

Briefly describe the cause of blind spots, and explain why writers must revise after writing.

PRACTICE

Turning passive voice verbs active is easy.

CHAPTER 3
EXERCISES

Exercise 8.

Rewrite each of these sentences, changing its passive voice verb to the active voice.

This will be killed by the reviewers in a New York minute.

____

Should the conference be attended by part-time employees?

____

Small gifts were exchanged by the delegates, and it was pledged they would meet again soon.

____

Our children are usually taught that most adults are kind and intelligent.

____

Recommended

____

____

____

____

PRACTICE

Active voice verbs tell more than passive.

Exercise 9.

Passive voice verbs rob your writing of precision by failing to tell *by whom.* The writer knows who did (or will do) what but cannot see that he or she is withholding this valuable information from the reader.

Rewrite the following passage in the active voice. BUT BEFORE YOU CAN, you need to know: The writer is reporting on a research project conducted for his or her company by Purdue University.

> *It is recommended that digital embedding be used, and it is believed that this can be done easily.*

Your Rewrite

____

____

____

Recommended

____

____

____

PRACTICE

Active vs. passive voice verbs.

Exercise 10.

Sometimes *by whom* is obvious or unimportant. Then the passive may be appropriate. Consider rewriting this passage in the active voice. (But you may want to leave it passive):

> *After the storm, victims were aided by both police and volunteers. The rainfall is believed to be the heaviest of any 24-hour period in the city's history.*

Your Rewrite

____

____

____

____

Recommended

____

____

____

____

PRACTICE

The passive voice is sometimes appropriate.

Exercise 11.

Decide whether the passive voice verb in each of the sentences below would be better in the active voice or should remain in the passive. Rewrite those you think should be active.

It was argued by the defense lawyers that DNA evidence is inconclusive.

Your order will be shipped June 28th.

Last year, an amount of sugar equal to his or her weight was consumed by the average American.

Recommended

PRACTICE

Mentioning people: You tell more.

Exercise 12.

Get people into your sentences. The writing will be more precise and sound more courteous. Don't introduce people artificially; simply don't go out of your way to block them out. Impersonal tone is no guarantee that you treated the subject objectively.

Try rewriting this passage in a more personal, sympathetic way. When you do, notice that making it warmer does not in any way affect the accuracy or dignity:

> *As of today's date, this office has succeeded in vacating 12 positions through retirement or reassignment. It is doubtful that an additional 20 positions can be similarly vacated before June 20.*
>
> *It is hoped at all cost that the laying off of any employees can be avoided. Any assistance that can be rendered in this matter will be appreciated by the writer.*

Your Rewrite

Recommended

PRACTICE

Write it the way you would say it.

Exercise 13.

Conversational style can be a guide to the best way of writing most things. It will often make your writing clearer and more gracious. The passage below is from the personnel department of a large hospital, but the principles of writing are the same regardless of the subject or the nature of the organization. Try writing this passage as you would say it if you were face to face with your reader:

> *Acknowledgment is made of your recent correspondence regarding employment opportunities available in this institution.*
>
> *Additional information is requested for proper evaluation of your credentials and career objectives. In this regard, an application for employment is enclosed together with a self-addressed envelope for your convenience. Upon receipt of the completed application, it will be reviewed and consideration will be based on openings relative to your qualifications. Should an opening compatible with those qualifications be available, you will be notified.*

Your Rewrite

Recommended

Caution: The listener will forgive a little carelessness, but the reader will not. You must be more careful in writing than in talking to keep the grammar entirely correct.

"My method is to take the utmost trouble to find the right thing to say, and then to say it with the utmost of levity."

—George Bernard Shaw

CHAPTER 4

CHANGING SOME OLD ATTITUDES

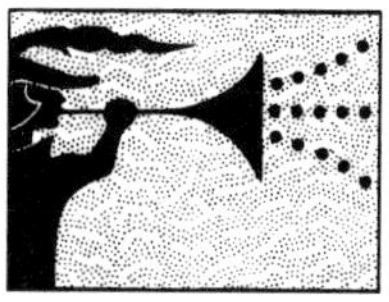

Languages change. Especially, the language of the United States and the British Commonwealth changes to suit the needs of the cultures it serves, as those cultures change. Languages also pick up strange, hard-to-explain traits, and people often have strong feelings about what is right or wrong usage in the language of their nurture.

Throughout their educations, most students in America's schools and universities spend more time studying English than any other subject. For the most part, however, that time is spent studying *literature.* We read. We study how others wrote. Might the designers and guardians of this method of teaching have thought that somehow we would learn to write by reading? It doesn't happen that way—any more than we learn to cook by eating. Most students passing through our education system have received very little specific advice on language usage and writing skills. (We see signs the emphasis is shifting in recent years, however, with more teaching devoted to composition.)

Our language (British and American) has changed drastically since much of our great literature was written. (For example, in Shakespeare's "Romeo, Romeo, wherefore art thou Romeo?" Juliet is not asking *Where are you, Romeo;* she is asking, *WHY are you Romeo*—a bit of self-pity. *(Why couldn't you have been someone else, so our families wouldn't be enemies and we could marry?)* In Elizabethan England, the time of Shakespeare (1564–1616), *wherefore* was the common word for *why,* and that is typical of the changes that have altered English through the centuries.) Gradually, as the language and culture continued to change in later centuries, much of the great earlier literature became so hard to read and understand that English teachers had to become specialists at explaining it. American literature fared better. Still today, however, most English teachers are literature specialists. And many hold up literary style as the model for writing style today.

All of us, however, received at least some exposure to the important rules of English usage. Unfortunately, many who pass through our education system also learn some well-intentioned but questionable pieces of advice along the way. These are usually negative—things we were told prudent writers just don't do.

Three in particular are so widespread almost every student has been exposed to them. We learn these as rules of grammar, or of composition. But these are misunderstandings and have never been rules, according to the scholars and outstanding writers who are considered today's authorities on English language usage. Let us expose the most common of these so-called rules and free all writers forever from the tyrrany of their restrictions.

The Three Taboos

TABOO NO. 1 *THAT YOU MAY NOT BEGIN SENTENCES WITH* ***AND*** *or* ***BUT.*** Of course you may. In fact, there are times you should. Here is why: These small but mighty words are called conjunctions, or *connectives.* What do they connect? Your ideas. And (oops!) what is the basic vehicle of the idea? *The sentence.* When someone advises us, then, that we may not begin sentences with *And* or *But,* we are deprived of the two most useful rhetorical devices for connecting the flow of logic from one sentence to the next. Two choices remain: We may have the smooth flow of the connective, **or** the clarity and efficiency of short sentences, but we may not have both. But (oops!) good writers refuse to make that choice. What can be wrong with short, smooth sentences? **Connectives allow you smooth, logical flow AND the clarity and impact of short sentences.**

Of course, do not go out of your way looking for opportunities to begin sentences with *And* or *But.* Rather, don't back off when doing so seems the natural thing to do. Here is an example in which a splendid writer felt beginning sentences with *And* and *But* was natural and desirable. *The Wall Street Journal* is regularly one of the best written publications in the United States:

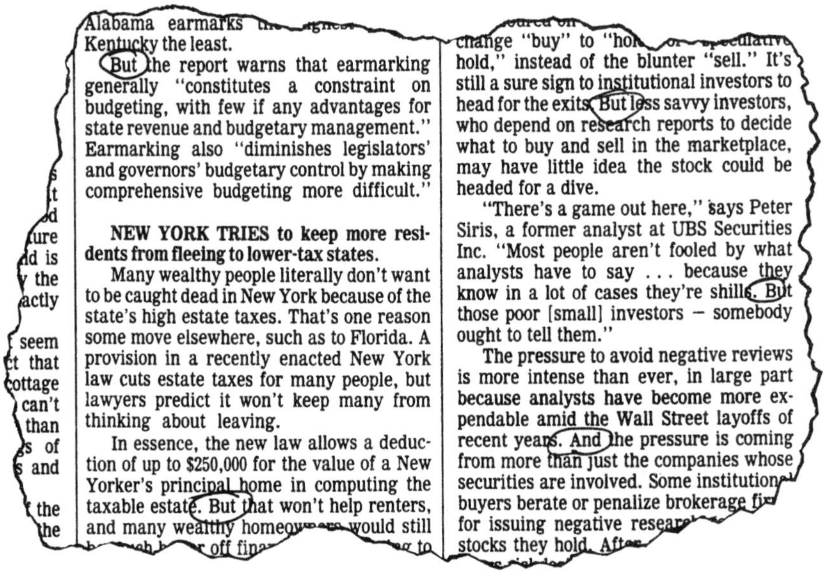

Alabama earmarks th... Kentucky the least.

But the report warns that earmarking generally "constitutes a constraint on budgeting, with few if any advantages for state revenue and budgetary management." Earmarking also "diminishes legislators' and governors' budgetary control by making comprehensive budgeting more difficult."

NEW YORK TRIES to keep more residents from fleeing to lower-tax states.

Many wealthy people literally don't want to be caught dead in New York because of the state's high estate taxes. That's one reason some move elsewhere, such as to Florida. A provision in a recently enacted New York law cuts estate taxes for many people, but lawyers predict it won't keep many from thinking about leaving.

In essence, the new law allows a deduction of up to $250,000 for the value of a New Yorker's principal home in computing the taxable estate. But that won't help renters, and many wealthy homeo... would still ...

... change "buy" to "ho... hold," instead of the blunter "sell." It's still a sure sign to institutional investors to head for the exits. But less savvy investors, who depend on research reports to decide what to buy and sell in the marketplace, may have little idea the stock could be headed for a dive.

"There's a game out here," says Peter Siris, a former analyst at UBS Securities Inc. "Most people aren't fooled by what analysts have to say ... because they know in a lot of cases they're shills. But those poor [small] investors – somebody ought to tell them."

The pressure to avoid negative reviews is more intense than ever, in large part because analysts have become more expendable amid the Wall Street layoffs of recent years. And the pressure is coming from more than just the companies whose securities are involved. Some institution... buyers berate or penalize brokerage fi... for issuing negative resear... stocks they hold. After...

The Wall Street Journal
(Dow Jones & Company, Inc., Publisher

You may be thinking, "*The Wall Street Journal* has literary freedom to bend the rules of grammar." But we are not encouraging you to bend or ignore rules of grammar—not even slightly. That would be most inappropriate. Our language has never had a rule against beginning sentences with *And* or *But.* Witness the following sample from the *Oxford English Dictionary,* acknowledged by scholars worldwide as the most respected authority on English usage:

> GENERAL EXPLANATIONS.
>
> THE VOCABULARY.
>
> THE Vocabulary of a widely-diffused and highly-cultivated living language is not a fixed quantity circumscribed by definite limits. That vast aggregate of words and phrases which constitutes the Vocabulary of English-speaking men presents, to the mind that endeavours to grasp it as a definite whole, the aspect of one of those nebulous masses familiar to the astronomer, in which a clear and unmistakable nucleus shades off on all sides, through zones of decreasing brightness, to a dim marginal film that seems to end nowhere, but to lose itself imperceptibly in the surrounding darkness. In its constitution it may be compared to one of those natural groups of the zoologist or botanist, wherein typical species forming the characteristic nucleus of the order, are linked on every side to other species, in which the typical character is less and less distinctly apparent, till it fades away in an outer fringe of aberrant forms, which merge imperceptibly in various surrounding orders, and whose own position is ambiguous and uncertain. For the convenience of classification, the naturalist may draw the line, which bounds a class or order, outside or inside of a particular form; but Nature has drawn it nowhere. So the English Vocabulary contains a nucleus or central mass of many thousand words whose 'Anglicity' is unquestioned; some of them only literary, some of them only colloquial, the great majority at once literary and colloquial,—they are the *Common Words* of the language. But they are linked on every side with other words which are less and less entitled to this appellation, and which pertain ever more and more distinctly to the domain of local dialect, of the slang and cant of 'sets' and classes, of the peculiar technicalities of trades and processes, of the scientific terminology common to all civilized nations, of the actual languages of other lands and peoples. And there is absolutely no defining line in any direction: the circle of the English language has a well-defined centre but no discernible circumference*. Yet practical utility has some bounds, and a Dictionary has definite limits: The lexicographer must, like the naturalist, 'draw the li[...]where', in each diverging direction. He

Oxford English Dictionary
(Oxford University Press, Publisher)

The curious thing about this taboo is that all of us who read see sentences every day beginning with *And* and *But.* But most readers probably never notice them. And that, incidentally, should be a powerful suggestion that if you use these little tools of grammar intelligently your readers will not notice, either.

As a matter of fact, if you are going to shorten sentences as we urged in Chapter 2, you will soon understand why connectives are so important a part of writing, serving as bridges between ideas, carrying your reader safely and logically from the end of one to the beginning of the next. True, as the English teacher says, they add nothing to the grammar. But they do add important *flow.* There is a logical meaning imparted by that little word *And.* (Flash: The next idea is related to and agrees with the last.) Still a different logical meaning imparted by *But.* (Flash: The next idea is related to but somehow conflicts with the last.) Other connectives are equally important; look for opportunities to begin sentences with words such as *Therefore, Next,* and *Still.* Do not deprive yourself of these important bridges from thought to thought. They alone can make the difference between a shaky and a skilled writer.

TABOO NO. 2 is at the ends of sentences: *THAT YOU MAY NOT END A SENTENCE WITH A PREPOSITION.* Again, of course you may. The alternative may be an awkward, unnatural sentence. We admit that prepositions are weak words. Therefore, when a sentence ends with one it tends to dribble to a close, like a bouncing ping-pong ball, rather than ending crisply. Still, that's sometimes a better choice than taking the long way around.

Probably the best known illustration of this point is a famous Winston Churchill story. Allegedly, while the great man was prime minister of England a junior officer criticized him for ending a sentence with a preposition, and the great man shot back: "*This is the type of arrant pedantry up with which I will not put.*" There we have the awkward, unnatural sentence as an alternative to ending with a preposition. If this story is true, Churchill (hero of England during World War II and author of the five-volume *A History of the English-Speaking Peoples*) would end with two prepositions.

The prejudice against ending sentences with prepositions seems to come, in some fuzzy way, from Latin. Fuzzy because Latin has no such restriction. (In fact, probably the most widely written or spoken phrase in the history of Western civilization is the liturgical, *Dominus vobiscum.* That's *God be with you,* and notice where the *cum* [*with*] is positioned.)

Even if Latin had such a restriction, to proclaim that it must therefore apply to English would be a remarkable nonsequitur. Ours is not one of the Romance (Latin-based) languages (Italian, French, Spanish, Portuguese, and Romanian), and Latin rules simply do not fit the Anglo-Saxon mold.

Avoid Clichés Like the Plague?

A cliché is a group of words used as a common expression, such as ". . . like the plague." Writers usually enjoy them because clichés are colorful. (Ironically, they become clichés because they are so expressive. For that same reason, they become corny from overuse.)

Another objection is that once they become popular the collective meaning may have little to do with the individual meanings of the words, and therefore there is no authorized definition of the cliché. How accurate are *ballpark figures*? They can be as accurate or inaccurate as the author would like; the reader has no way of knowing.

What is the meaning of the statement, "Phone your customers *on a daily basis*."? Phone them every

TABOO NO. 3 is probably the most restrictive of all: *THAT YOU MAY NOT REPEAT WORDS.* (We call this belief "**The Elongated Yellow Fruit Sickness,**" named for all the writers who can never call a *banana* a *banana* the second time.) You may have been advised, "Use a word once. If you need it again, or at least if you need it very soon, it's prudent to seek a synonym instead." This is truly damaging advice.

The issue here is *first-choice words.* When an intelligent person selects a particular word—either intuitively or after careful thought to keep the writing clear—that selection is probably a reasonable endorsement of this particular word, and no other, as the first-choice word for that particular situation.

You are told to seek a different word for variety. But our objectives in choosing words are *clarity and precision*—not variety. If your first-choice word was the correct one, but now you believe you must use something else to express that same thought, you go to a second-, third-, or fourth-choice word. Rather, reuse the first-choice one. Thoughtful writers usually attain all the variety readers need through the changing information flow of the subjects and the situations they write about.

Again our literary giant for the defense is Winston Churchill. In the early years of World War II, when invasion of England by the powerful German armies seemed only days away, he electrified the world, and lifted the spirits of the heavily bombed British people and gave them the will to fight, in a radio speech that can still be heard today. The words were:

> "We shall fight them on the beaches, we shall fight them on the landing grounds, we shall fight them in the fields and in the streets, we shall fight in the hills; we shall never surrender."

Few exact synonyms are found in English; you usually go from specific to abstract when you seek them; the abstract word may offer a choice of several specific meanings. Therefore the writing becomes less precise.

Another danger is that you may mislead the reader by switching words. He or she may not realize you intended the two words to mean the same thing. For example, suppose you are writing about a microscope. If you cannot use the word *microscope* again, you might refer to it as the *instrument* the second time. That could mean almost anything. And the third time you might refer to it as the *unit.* Now you have switched signals (twice) without warning the reader. Little irregularities such as this can derail the flow of information from your brain to the reader's.

Unit, incidentally, is one of the most awkwardly used words in the English language. Use it only when you are referring to units of measure, such as unit price or unit package. But do not use *unit* as a universal synonym for all nouns. Used that way, a unit is an academic *whatchamacallit.*

By all means repeat first-choice words. Remember, the objectives when you are choosing words should be clarity and precision—not variety. *When you use second-, third-, or fourth-choice words, you are hurting your reader by causing images to become blurred.*

To avoid *too much* repetition, the language gives us pronouns. You may refer to the microscope as *it* or to two or more as *they.* Of course, you can do this only after establishing what *it* or *they* stands for, by using the original word first. Putting this grammatically, pronouns need antecedents. Use pronouns as naturally in your writing as you would in conversation.

Let us repeat this important point about grammar, to prevent any possible misunderstanding. Although this book encourages writers to embrace some enlightened attitudes toward our language as that language changes, please do not form the impression that grammar is no longer important. Correct grammar is essential—as important today as it ever has been. But grammar should not inhibit us. Most educated adults should have no trouble keeping their grammar correct unless they allow sentences to become dangerously long and complicated. Good writing is easy to read and sounds natural. In expository writing, style should not call attention to itself; the language does its job best by staying in the background, holding your ideas up for all to see. When you feel that beginning a sentence with a connective, or ending with a preposition, or repeating a good word seems natural or desirable, don't hesitate to do so. In these cases the ideas will flow so smoothly that readers are unlikely to notice you did a few things some of them may have been taught are wrong. *Remember, too, these three taboos are* ***not*** *rules of grammar and never have been.*

Two other things you should not have been told: Consider yourself lucky if no one ever advised you **that you may not mix verb tenses.** Posh and piffle! (Perhaps even: Pshaw!) How else could you say something like, "*Goodman called (past tense) this morning and is wondering (present) when the Starlight order will be delivered (future).*"

Nor should writers listen seriously when someone argues **that a paragraph must contain at least two sentences.** The rationale here is questionable and inflexible: that a paragraph is a cluster of related sentences, and there

day? Return their calls within 24 hours?

What is the precise meaning of *leveling the playing field?*

Still another objection is that in their eagerness to use clichés people often get the words wrong. *I could care less* should be *I couldn't care less.* (You already care so little it would not be possible to care less.) Or: *Each one was better than the next.* That really means they got progressively worse. Is that what the author intended?

In spite of these shortcomings, writing without occasional clichés would probably be impossible and not worth the effort. You needn't, therefore, avoid them *like the plague.*

But if you can avoid one as easily as saying . . . *as you would avoid catching a deadly disease,* you probably should.

cannot be a cluster of one. Good writing usually doesn't thrive in an environment of rigid thinking. A very short sentence, in fact, can be a wonderfully effective paragraph, making a powerful statement, drawing the reader's eye because it stands out from the longer paragraphs that surround it. (For more on paragraphs, see page 139.)

How Important Is Brevity?

From our discussion so far, you may have the impression that good writing should be as brief as possible. Not so. In fact, that may be a risky attitude.

Although brevity in writing is desirable, conveying your message accurately and clearly is far more important—the reason you write. The experienced writer knows that readers are more interested in reading *comfort* than in overall length, and if they do care about length they measure it in reading time, not number of pages or words. To your reader, then, brevity is more a function of clarity and organizing properly than of total length. (As we have already said, Part 2 of this book will discuss organizing.)

Fortunately, in most cases the same characteristics that make writing clear also make it brief. The advice on brevity, then, is: **seek clarity, and the brevity will come.** But if you seek deliberately to be as brief as possible, two things may go wrong. First, you may leave out important information in your zeal to keep the writing short. Second, you may end up sounding blunt, by stripping the writing of those courtesy words that create the image you are a courteous and open-minded human being. You become far less *persuasive* as a result. Phrases of good will such as "*Will you please . . .*" and "*We would be grateful if . . .*" add little to the length of a letter, and their absence certainly has negative impact—especially in a letter. They are a wise investment.

Thoughtful writers do try hard to get rid of padding—to trim the fat without hurting the meat. But they do not, and you should not, try to strip the writing down to the bare minimum of words. Prudent, intelligent authors ought to be able to trim just enough but not too much—to keep their writing moving at an interesting pace but not too fast.

By all means learn to recognize wasted words and knock them swiftly out of your writing. Some words add absolutely nothing but length; they are just there, contributing no meaning, no emphasis, no courtesy. They creep in because the author is too lazy to block them out. Sometimes they are worse than wasted; they may make the author sound silly, as in the following passage:

> . . . you, if interested in making this acquisition, must do so on the basis that you will not, in all probability, enjoy the tax advantages which the present owners have been obtaining from the multiple corporate setup. Past experience shows that the Internal Revenue Service would take action to disallow the claiming of tax benefits resulting from the use of multiple corporations insofar as they are established primarily for that purpose. We were advised by Mr. Green that the multiple corporate setup had been started a number of years ago not to reduce taxes but in an effort to avoid being subject to the wage and. . . . (34 words)

There you see wasted words that make the author look silly. Like ***past*** *experience.* Is there any other kind? Likewise *take action to, the claiming of,* and *insofar as* add nothing. Without them, the passage says the same thing but in one-third fewer words:

. . . you, if interested in making this acquisition, must do so on the basis that you will not, in all probability, enjoy the tax advantages which the present owners have been obtaining from the multiple corporate setup. Experience shows that the Internal Revenue Service would disallow tax benefits resulting from the use of multiple corporations established primarily for that purpose. We were advised by Mr. Green that the multiple corporate setup had been started a number of years ago not to reduce taxes but in an effort to avoid being subject to the wage and. . . . (23 words)

But not every word without precise meaning is wasted. Thoughtful authors sometimes insert a word or phrase just for emphasis. You may have noticed, for example, the statement a few paragraphs above (page 56): "Some words add absolutely nothing but length." It's true that *absolutely* adds nothing to the meaning. It adds emphasis, however. The statement is more forceful than if it just said "Some words add nothing but length."

Another habit that adds unnecessary length to writing—and also makes it less interesting—is the tendency to turn verbs into nouns. One of the surest ways to make any statement slow moving, and dull, is to rob its verbs of strength by turning them into other parts of speech. Verbs are action words. More than any other part of speech, therefore, they keep the ideas moving. But some writers, as though seeking to bore readers, turn desirable verbs into nouns, then rearrange the sentence so its verb becomes *is* or something equally uninspiring. Here is an example of that type of extra-long and extra-dull writing. Notice how some key words are weakened:

Utilization of the computer for the management of heating and ventilation will bring about a reduction in fuel costs. (15 words)

Here is that same passage again, shorter and clearer, the way most people would like to read it:

Using the computer to manage heating and ventilation will reduce fuel costs. (10 words)

We repeat: Brevity is desirable, but clarity is more important. Seek clarity and the brevity will come. By all means get rid of wasted words, but do not sacrifice useful information in a quest to be brief. Also remember, stripping writing to the bone will usually cause the tone to suffer—to become blunt, overbearing. Courtesy is important in almost any endeavor, and a pleasant, dignified image—perhaps even charm if you wish to call it that—should be a standard part of your writing. Your image and credibility are at stake.

DEVIL'S ADVOCATE: Setting up conflicts with readers isn't my idea of what writers should want to do. Okay, let's say the enlightened reader knows that the three taboos are just misunderstandings, not rules. But most people think . . . and you agreed they do . . . that it's wrong to begin sentences with conjunctions, or end with prepositions. I'm going to look like a jerk in their eyes.

GURU: Do this to convince doubters, and to make yourself feel unjerked. Ask the doubter to open any book *by a writer he or she respects,* to any page at random, then bet an ice cream cone you'll find at least one sentence beginning with *and* or *but* on that page. You will almost always win. The point is, that person, like all of us, has been reading similar sentences every day of his or her life *but hasn't noticed them because they're so natural.* Why, then, are you worried people will notice yours? Bet someone an expensive dinner on any given day that you'll find at least 10 sentences beginning with *and* or *but* on page 1 of that day's *Wall Street Journal.* You can have a free dinner with someone new every night.

DEVIL'S ADVOCATE: But I'm not going to . . .

GURU: See? You just did it!

DEVIL'S ADVOCATE: (Sigh.) But I'm not going to be there to do that bet to reassure my readers.

GURU: Well, bet *yourself* against *The Wall Street Journal* for that expensive dinner. The point is, if *you* haven't noticed these things as a reader, can't you relax and assume your readers don't notice them either? But you raise a thoughtful point: Don't go out of your way to exercise this new freedom with *and* or *but.* If you begin sentences with them too often, your reader may indeed notice and think less of you.

DEVIL'S ADVOCATE: Why not begin sentences with *also* and *however* when connectives are needed, instead of *and* or *but?*

GURU: You can. These are actually conjunctive adverbs, not pure conjunctions. Because they're adverbs, they modify the verb, and so the writer gets the choice of placing them at the beginning of the sentence (*However, they soon realized this was unsafe* . . .), or in the middle, next to the verb (*They soon realized, however, this was unsafe* . . .) or at the end (*They soon realized this was unsafe, however.*)

DEVIL'S ADVOCATE: Please clarify the correct attitude about repeating first choice words. If writers shouldn't use synonyms instead, what's the point of Roget's Thesaurus?

GURU: Poor Monsieur Roget. He must look down from that great literary enclave in the sky and wonder repeatedly how it came about that so many thoughtful people have misunderstood the purpose of his great work. When you seek synonyms, you're moving from first choice words to second, third, and sometimes fourth choice. You're going backward. Why? Use a thesaurus to find a *first choice* word when you know the one you have isn't quite it.

CHAPTER 4

REVIEW

What is another word for conjunctions?

____

Writers should sometimes begin sentences with them so readers can have the benefit of ________________ *and* ________________.

List other useful connectives, besides **and** *and* **but.**

____

____

For what reason should writers feel free to end sentences with prepositions?

____

____

Synonyms are usually used as ____________________ *words.*

What are the dangers of seeking them rather than repeating words?

____

____

On trying to be brief, the sensible advice is:
Seek ________________, *and the* ________________ *will come.*

What two things may go wrong if you try to write in the fewest possible words?

____

____

Skillful writers try to avoid changing verbs to nouns (often ending with **-tion***)*
because: ____________________________________

____

How alert were you? All of these important questions were discussed in the chapter you just read. You should be able to answer them all. If you cannot, you are urged to look them up.

PRACTICE

Smooth flow through connectives.

CHAPTER 4

EXERCISES

Exercise 14.

One of the surest and easiest ways to improve your writing is to avoid long, complex sentences. But shortening sentences may cause the ideas to sound choppy unless you do something to restore the smooth, logical flow between the end of one idea and the beginning of the next. That is why connectives are so important—especially at the beginnings of sentences. There has never been any rule against beginning sentences with *and* or *but.*

Rewrite this passage, keeping both the clarity and impact of short sentences and the smooth logical flow of the connective:

> *Formerly, laser assemblies from Hungary could be installed on-line immediately if they matched current specifications, but now, different locations have different requirements, and these sometimes change without warning, making delays and complaints an everyday happening and the new color coding, although it seemed like a good idea when we approved it, is causing further delays.*

Your Rewrite

Recommended

PRACTICE
Logical flow through connectives.

Exercise 15.

Here is a serious grammar mistake in a memo from a social services agency. The writer probably made it because he or she tried to break the ideas in a long sentence, but without a connective. Rewriting the passage should be easy:

> *While it is not possible to keep everyone advised of changes in scheduled events sponsored by the various civic and religious organizations immediately as they occur. We try to keep all groups using the sound stage informed of changes that may affect them.*

Your Rewrite

Recommended

PRACTICE

The hidden danger of synonyms.

Exercise 16.

Seeking synonyms, rather than repeating first-choice words, may cause imprecision. There are few exact synonyms; your second-choice word is usually more general. Even if you do find an exact synonym, using two different words to describe the same thing may mislead your reader; he or she may think you are referring to two different things.

The result will probably be confusion, as in this letter from a sales executive to a customer. The poor synonyms are underlined. Try to rewrite the letter without them. But be careful:

> *Dear Mr. Fernhill,*
>
> *As you probably know, the 59th Annual Convention of the National Ice Cream Manufacturers and Dealers Association was held in New York City January 7th through 11th. Our company conducted a seminar at the meeting, on organization of retail stores and the use of computers.*
>
> *Because Fern-Pré Products was unable to have a member present at this event, I thought you might like to review our presentation. We have reproduced it in the enclosed brochure, reprinted from the official proceedings of the exposition published by the Society.*
>
> *We will be happy to provide you extra copies of this publication, if you would like them for other members of your management.*

Your Rewrite

(Continued on next page)

EXERCISE 16 Your rewrite (continued):

Recommended

PRACTICE
Stamp out wasted words!

Exercise 17.

Good writers are aware that clear expression usually ends up brief. But if you try deliberately to make the writing as short as possible, you may leave out ideas; or you may sound blunt, overbearing. Still, good writers learn to recognize and avoid wasted words—to trim the fat without hurting the meat. Try to recognize the wasted words in this passage and rewrite it without them:

> *While there is no time deadline placed on this project, it seems that a period of approximately two months should be adequately long. It would appear to me that one possible approach to this task would be for someone from your office to visit with Mr. Gellert and find out exactly what his needs and requirements are and then submit an action plan listing in detail the steps necessary to accomplish fully the objectives set out in Mr. Sauer's letter.*

Your Rewrite

Recommended

Exercise 18.

Content, not tone, makes writing official, or professional, or dignified. The tone of your letters and reports should at all times be pleasant yet courteous. Usually, the Six Principles of Clear Writing will create that tone. In fact, the quest to sound *official* or *professional* often makes writing dull and much too long.

Government letters and reports are often that way; we describe their style as *bureaucratic* or *gobbledygook.* Here is such a letter. But as you try to rewrite it, remember that professional men and women, scholars, engineers, and scientists write their share of gobbledygook too, just as hard to follow as this:

> *Monthly checks issued through this agency bear a duly authorized payment date of the 3rd of the month inasmuch as we are assigned that date under a staggered check issuance arrangement in affect among the various Federal agencies which issue monthly checks. The purpose, of course, is to avoid some of the cyclic difficulties that post offices, the Treasury Department, and other institutions would encounter if all Federal checks were mailed or made payable simultaneously each month.*
>
> *Delivery of checks in advance of their payment dates creates further problems. On those occasions when checks were inadvertently released by a post office prior to the scheduled payment date, banks and other business institutions experienced certain difficulties, brought about when payees presented the instruments, marked payable as of the 3rd of the month, on the 2nd or earlier, in effect placing the business institution in the position of either honoring an illegal instrument or declining to do so and thereby antagonizing the payee.*
>
> *This office is pleased to report, however, that appropriate arrangements have been made with the Post Office and Treasury Department to have checks issued through this agency delivered henceforth on the 2nd of the month whenever the 3rd is a Sunday or holiday. This should, it would seem, accomplish the result you had in mind.*

Rewriting that letter will demand that you call on your imagination to fill in much missing information. Would any readers take that trouble? (Incidentally, did you notice a misused word?)

Your Rewrite

(Continued on next page)

PRACTICE
Clear writing first demands clear thinking.

EXERCISE 18 Your rewrite (continued):

Recommended

CHAPTER 5

MEASURING READABILITY

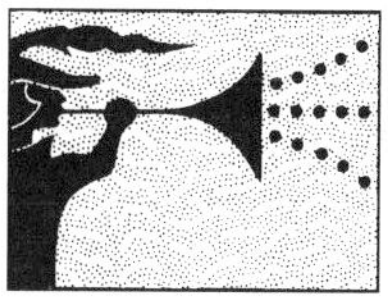

We come away feeling rewarded and refreshed after reading a good book or magazine article and absorbing something thought provoking—or entertaining. Conversely, frustration gives way to surrender when we try to read—want to understand—something but somehow *"just can't get into it."* The difference is often in the writing style. To an important degree, the writer determines how well readers will read. He or she controls the characteristics of writing that, in turn, influence every reader's ability to receive and understand.

Most people associate easy-to-understand writing with commonplace subjects, and as the subject becomes more difficult, so, they assume, must the reading. We have seen it that way most of our lives. What may be new to many is: Even *extremely difficult* information can be written in clear, relaxed English. (But doing so requires that the writer's *thinking* process is thorough.) In fact, those extra-hard subjects are the ones that most need easy-to-read language if readers are to understand. Is there a contradiction here?

If we examine the reader's needs, we arrive at this important guideline—a change of attitude for many writers:

> The more difficult the ideas, the easier the words and sentences should be, in order for their precious cargo of information to be received (understood) fully and accurately.

We see proof of this aspect of the writing→reading relationship every time we read *something we already know*. In these cases, even if the writing *style* is unclear we have no trouble reading with comprehension, because we aren't required to spend any reader energy trying to understand the subject; unless the writing style is outrageously bad, we can figure out the message.

ANOTHER WAY OF SAYING THIS: The more challenging your ideas may be, the more you, the writer (who already know them), should try to help your reader (who doesn't know them and is relying on your words and sentences to identify and understand them).

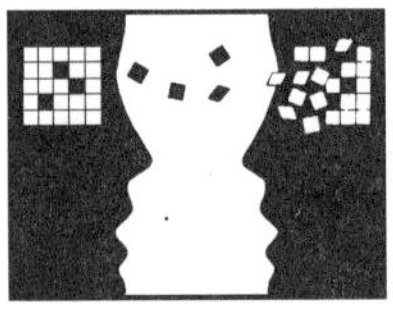

The Reading Process

Here is why: Reading, like writing, consumes body energy and can be a tiring process. The Reading Process takes place in fundamentally the opposite order of The Writing Process. (Writers encode; readers decode.) *First, the readerbrain receives black marks on a page—images of words and sentences—and converts these into meaningful concepts in the form of electrical energy. Second, it intelligently examines, sorts, combines, and stores (assimilates) those concepts.* Again, that vital separation—the total separation between WHAT is written and HOW it is written, or the IDEAS the reader receives and the WORDS AND SENTENCES through which he or she receives them.

At any given moment, a reader brings to the task a given amount of energy, and it must be divided those two ways. First, words and sentences (decoding); they will consume whatever amount of the reader's energy they demand. Whatever amount is left is available for the ideas—for comprehension (understanding) to take place.

What does this mean to us as writers? Put yourself for a moment in the reader's position. Imagine someone writes you a very simple message, such as: *"That lasagna was terrible"*—but in words so difficult and sentence structure so hard to follow that the decoding process demands, let's say, 95 percent of your available readerbrain energy at that moment. If this IDEA is so uncomplicated that it needs only 5 percent (or less) for comprehension, you can consume that 95 percent on words and sentences without risk. Comprehension *will* take place; communication will succeed. But trouble is ahead if the message is more complex—if the writer transmits his or her information in words and sentences demanding 95 percent of the reader's energy (for decoding), *and the information demands as much as 6 percent.* Now communication cannot fully succeed unless the reader works extraordinarily hard. Even if he or she tries, however, the readerbrain may lack energy to do the whole job, and part of the message will not be received, or will be misunderstood.

This reader energy shortage becomes especially critical if the writer hopes to convey extremely difficult information—for example, explaining the importance of the quantum mechanics theory of Max Planck and Werner Karl Heisenberg, or the reason your health care plan is being changed. Now if the full and accurate transfer of knowledge is to take place, the writer *must* keep the language workload as low as possible, because now the reader will need to reserve most of that energy for the *meaning.*

The more energy your reader must devote to words and sentences, the less is available for comprehension of the ideas. But the reading brain cannot decide how that energy will be divided; the writer decides this for the reader, because he or she chooses those words and builds them into grammatical structures called sentences.

Thoughtful writers need to be aware of this writerbrain/readerbrain relationship. Thoughtful writers should care whether their work will succeed in its goal, transferring knowledge. Therefore, thoughtful writers should ask of their writing habits: "How can I tell? How can I measure whether my language usage will help or hinder readers?" It is for this aspect of writing that linguists and reading specialists have given us ways, based on respected research, to measure readability.

Do Periods and Commas Go Inside or Outside Quotation Marks?

Always inside. There are no exceptions.

Other punctuation marks may go inside or outside, depending on how they are used. Determining is easy.

Place them INSIDE when they apply only to the matter being quoted: *McCarthy asked, "Has the character generator been repaired yet?"*

Place marks other than periods and commas OUTSIDE the quotation marks when they apply to more than just the matter being quoted: *Why did Doherty say, "Not everyone needs to follow this procedure"?*

Another useful tip on quotation marks: For quotations running several paragraphs, use quotation marks to open every paragraph but to close only the last paragraph of the quoted matter.

How hard is this passage to read?

share. The Indenture requires the redemption at par of $890,000 principal amount of debentures (less credits for converted debentures) each year beginning 1998, authorizes the optimal redemption at par of an additional $890,000 principal amount of debentures in each year (non-cumulative) beginning in 1993 and further optional redemptions at any time at prices ranging from $105.375 to $100.25, until 2008 and at par thereafter.

Loan agreements requiring the Company and its subsidiaries to maintain a consolidated net working capital, as defined in the credit agreement of September 16, 1994 of not less than $8,000,000 and limiting dividends, except in capital stock of the Company, and stock payments subsequent to December 31, 1993 to the consolidated net income accumulated after that date plus $500,000 (approximately $2,061,000 unrestricted at December 31, 1995) necessitated long-term borrowing in the amount of $3,750,000 to correct the deficiency of approximately $350,000 in working capital as of December 31, 1995.

The loan agreements also provide for restrictions on the declaration of dividends, stock payments and certain capital expenditures if net working capital, as defined in the credit agreement of September 16, 1994, is or would be less than $10,000,000.

Note D—Shares of Common Stock increased by 24,302 shares in 1995 through the issuance of a 3% stock dividend. Earned Surplus was charged in the amount of $559,858, representing $549.833 fair market value of stock issued and $10,025 paid in cash in lieu of fractional shares, and capital stock and capital surpl[illegible] credited for $121,000 and $4[illegible]

How easy is this one?

168 THE HUMAN BRAIN

The brain is highly demanding in another fashion. It uses up a great deal of oxygen in the course of its labors. In fact, in the resting body, 1/4 of the oxygen being consumed by the tissues is used up in the brain, although that organ makes up only 1/50 of the mass of the body. The consumption of oxygen involves the oxidation of the simple sugar (glucose) brought to the brain by the bloodstream. The brain is sensitive to any shortage of either oxygen or glucose and will be damaged by that shortage sooner than any other tissue. (It is the brain that fails first in death by asphyxiation. And it is the brain that fails in the baby if its first breath is unduly delayed.) The flow of blood through the brain is therefore carefully controlled by the body and is less subject to fluctuation than is the blood flow through any other organ. What is more, although it is easy to cause the blood vessels in the brain to dilate by use of drugs, it is impossible to make them constrict and thus cut down the blood supply.

The existence of a tumor can destroy the blood-brain barrier in the region of the tumor. This has its fortunate aspect. A drug labeled with a radioactive iodine atom and injected into the bloodstream will pass into the brain only at the site of the tumor and collect there.

THE CEREBRAL CORTEX

The Human Brain—Its Capacities and Functions
Isaac Asimov (Houghton Mifflin Company, publisher)

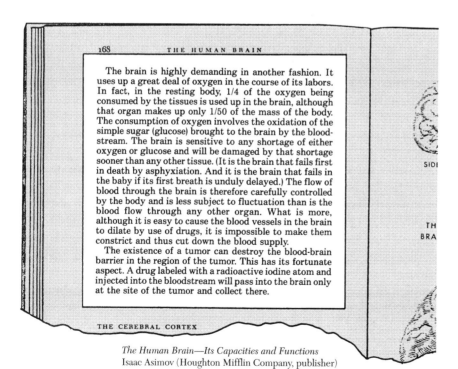

How the Experts Measure

Linguists in the past half century and experts in the teaching of reading have given us ways to measure the readability of a piece of writing—how easy or difficult it is to read. That is, the *language workload* it imposes on readers. (This is unrelated to the difficulty of the ideas.) Language too simple or too difficult might create barriers—resistance to understanding. Educators often use this kind of information in choosing books for students in different school grade levels. (And for that reason, publishers also care about readability levels.) As a caring writer, you too should want this valuable information about your relationship with your readers.

Most systems for measuring readability concentrate on two language characteristics: How familiar are the words, and how helpful are the grammatical structures (sentences). The systems differ in the ways they measure these.

Word processing programs often contain a subprogram, based on the linguists' findings, that measures those same characteristics, and any one of several of these can tell writers how they're doing *while they are writing into the computer.* The methods of analyzing are based on two reasonably safe generalizations: That small words create less resistance to understanding than large ones, and that sentences of moderate length help the flow of ideas more than extremely short or extremely long ones do. As *generalizations,* these are easily shown to be statistically valid.

Word difficulty. Linguists call large words *polysyllables,* and most readability researchers define a polysyllable as any word having three syllables or more. *For statistical measurement only,* one- or two-syllable words are counted easy; words of three or more syllables are difficult. (NOTE that dramatic exceptions to this rule are found throughout any dictionary. *Id,* for example, is an exceptionally short word yet exceptionally difficult; *transportation* is the opposite. In English [but not all languages], if the line separating easy and difficult is drawn after the second syllable, exceptions on either side of that line occur in about equal frequency. They can be ignored, therefore, because the exceptions cancel each other mathematically.)

Analysis of the writing of 16,000 adults* reveals that normal (non-specialized) writing or speech *on general (non-specialized) subjects* usually contains between 10 and 15 percent polysyllables. Specialized fields (engineering, medicine, law, etc.) occasionally require terms common only to that profession and therefore may need as high as 20 percent polysyllables (but rarely higher).

Sentence difficulty. A writing style in which sentences average between 15 and 20 words in length seems helpful to most readers. Occasional sentences may be as short as 2 or 3 words, or as long as 30 or 35†, and a *variety* of lengths keeps readers alert and comfortable. (See Chapter 3.) These limits provide a vast amount of literary freedom—enough to satisfy the artistic needs of any writer. More important, they satisfy the needs of that person at the receiving end: your reader.

DoubleWHAT?

Have you ever wondered why the letter W is pronounced doubleyou, not doublevee?

---

*By the author, in classroom measurements of students' own writing.

† Very skilled writers may occasionally write longer ones.

Evaluating Your Own Writing

How to measure. These two characteristics, then, word difficulty and sentence difficulty, together form the *language workload* readers must deal with during the reading process. Some writers seem able to sense and control the level of that workload intuitively while they write; others look for simple, reliable ways, at least occasionally, to confirm this part of their skills.

Using those factors that linguists and reading authorities use, you can measure the readability of a passage of writing in three steps:

1. In a sample (100 to 200 words) of any writing, figure the *average* number of words per sentence. (The sample should begin and end at a period.)
2. In that sample, figure the *percentage* of polysyllables. (Count any word of three or more syllables as a polysyllable. Also any number containing five or more digits, unless the ending digits are all 0's.)
3. Add those numbers together.

Their total is the readability index of that passage, based on measurement of the factors that most influence language workload (as opposed to *subject* workload).

EXAMPLE: (Step 1.) If a passage has 148 words, and they are divided into 8 sentences, the average sentence length is 18.5 words (148 ÷ 8). Without further figuring, you have learned that in this sample the author divides ideas into sentences of reasonable length. (Step 2.) If 16 of those 148 words are polysyllables, that is 10.8 percent (16 ÷ 148—divide the large number into the small one.) Then: (Step 3.) 18.5 + 10.8 = Readability index 29.3, or 29.

What should it be? For adult readers, strive for a readability index between 25 and 30. Anything between 20 and 35 is probably acceptable, but the 25–30 range is likely to present your information in its most readable form. Under 20, a childish tone may distract readers and interfere with the flow of logic. If the total of vocabulary workload and sentence workload is over 40, the style is almost certainly unreadable for sustained reading.

The passage below is from Herman Melville's great novel, *Moby Dick.* It contains 363 words divided into 8 sentences, averaging 20 words per sentence. Of those 363 words, 27 (or 7 percent) are polysyllables. The readability index of the passage, then, is a very unchallenging 27:

READABILITY INDEX

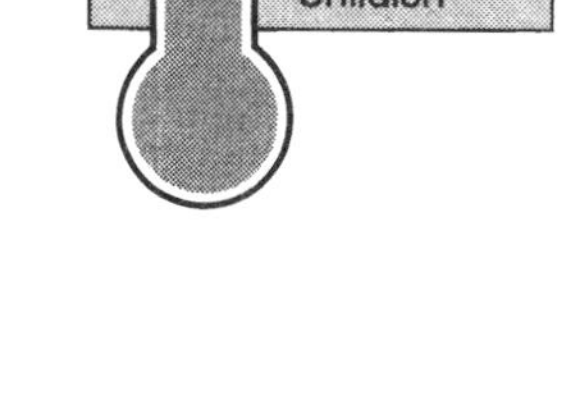

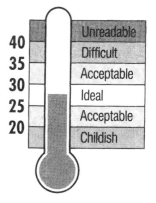

In the tumultuous business of cutting-in and attending to a whale, there is much running backwards and forwards among the crew. Now hands are wanted here, and then again hands are wanted there. There is no staying in any one place; for at one and the same time everything has to be done everywhere. It is much the same with him who endeavors the description of the scene. We must now retrace our way a little. It was mentioned that upon first breaking ground in the whale's back, the blubber-hook was inserted into the original hole there cut by the spades of the mates. But how did so clumsy and weighty a mass as that same hook get fixed in that hole? It was inserted there by my particular friend Queequeg, whose duty it was, as harpooneer, to descent upon the monster's back for the special purpose referred to. But in very many cases, circumstances require that the harpooneer shall remain on the whale till the whole flensing or stripping operation is concluded. The whale, be it observed, lies almost entirely submerged, excepting the immediate parts operated upon. So down there, some ten feet below the level of the deck, the poor harpooneer flounders about, half on the whale and half in the water, as the vast mass revolves like a treadmill beneath him. On the occasion in question, Queequeg figured in the Highland costume—a shirt and socks—in which to my eyes, at least, he appeared to uncommon advantage; and no one had a better chance to observe him, as will presently be seen.

Being the savage's bowman, that is, the person who pulled the bow-oar in his boat (the second one from forward), it was my cheerful duty to attend upon him while taking that hard-scrabble scramble upon the dead whale's back. You have seen Italian organ-boys holding a dancing-ape by a long cord. Just so, from the ship's steep side, did I hold Queequeg down there in the sea, by what is technically called in the fishery a monkey-rope, attached to a strong strip of canvas belted around his waist.

It was a humorously perilous business for both of us.

Moby Dick
Herman Melville (E.P. Dutton & Co., publisher)

Pratt's Law

In large organizations such as government agencies, several people may have to approve everything you write. This requirement can cause trouble, because they may not agree on what is or is not good writing. In fact, they may contradict each other.

Disagreement is especially common over the amount of detail a writer should include. The poor public servant may try to please his or her boss by including as much supporting information as possible in a report.

That boss may be pleased, but the next one up the line says, "Too much detail . . . burdens the reader . . . the chief will never approve this." The poor PS, then, removes the details, but the next boss up says, "Not enough data; the conclusions are unsupported." And so on.

At the Central Intelligence Agency, writers developed Pratt's Law as a guideline:

"Whether you should include a large or small amount of details depends on whether there will be an even or odd number of reviewers."

(Also see: Reviewing and Editing the Writing of Others, page 147.)

(BUT NOTE that not all of Melville's work is that readable. The vocabulary throughout *Moby Dick* is unchallenging, but some passages contain sentences so long that readers must strain to follow an idea from capital letter to period. Some of his other works were described by his publisher as ". . . all but unreadable."

Analyzing your strengths and weaknesses. The Readability Index is a most useful tool. Use it to measure how clearly you have written. But you can use it also to analyze *while* you are writing, to learn some valuable things about your writing habits. What are your strengths and weaknesses? What must you do to get rid of the weaknesses?

Remember, any combination of Steps 1 and 2 totaling between 25 and 30 is at a proper workload level.

Suppose, for example, in analyzing a passage you count 15 words per sentence and 15 percent polysyllables. Or 22 words per sentence and 8 percent polysyllables. Both total 30. You can give the reader any combination totaling 30—even 25 words per sentence and 5 percent polysyllables, or 5 words per sentence and 25 percent polysyllables. (At 25 words per sentence and 5 percent polysyllables, in effect readers are receiving easy information in large doses; at 5 words per sentence and 25 percent polysyllables, the vocabulary is dangerously burdensome but is delivered in mercifully small doses.)

In some cases you may not be able to control the vocabulary workload. You can always, however, control sentence length. If a particular subject requires a heavy vocabulary workload, compensate by shortening sentences. Balancing the factors of the language workload this way will make a great difference in whether the reader understands your ideas.

BUT CAUTION: All readability formulas have one limitation. Regardless of what method you use, there is much about writing we cannot measure in numbers. The method given here provides a statistically reliable measure of how difficult the sentences are, but it cannot measure whether the ideas progress logically from sentence to sentence, or even whether the grammar is correct. It does measure, quite reliably according to linguists and educators, how hard the words are, but no formula can measure if they were the right words in the first place.

It may be useful to compare a readability formula to a fever thermometer. The thermometer measures only *one* health sign, not all. Still, no doctor would begin a medical examination without that information. Too high or too low a body temperature tells us something is wrong, but a temperature of 98.6 degrees certainly does not tell us the patient is healthy. Likewise, too high or too low a readability index tells us something is wrong, but an index of 30 does not ensure good writing. No developer of a readability formula ever claimed otherwise. (This paragraph and the one before it have a readability index of 33.5.)

If you accept that limitation, a readability formula may be useful in telling you some important things about your writing. Remember however, these formulas measure *HOW* you write, not *WHAT* you write.

The following research report, from the National Aeronautics and Space Administration, illustrates that total separation. It has a readability index of 61—totally unreadable. After it, a simpler version presents the exact same ideas with a very moderate index of 29. Here is the difficult (original) version:

An experimental performance evaluation of a 6.02-inch tip diameter radial-inflow turbine utilizing argon as the working fluid was made over a range of inlet total pressure from 1.2 to 9.4 pounds per square inch absolute with corresponding Reynolds number from 20,000 to 225,000. (Reynolds number, as applied herein, is definable as the ratio of the weight flow to the product of viscosity and rotor tip radius, where the viscosity is determined at the turbine entrance conditions.) Efficiency and equivalent weight flow increased with increasing inlet pressure and Reynolds number. At design equivalent speed and pressure ratio, total efficiency increased from 0.85 to 0.90 and static efficiency from 0.80 to 0.84 with increasing Reynolds number, while the corresponding increase in equivalent weight flow was approximately 2 percent. The relationship established between experimentally determined efficiency and corresponding Reynolds number indicated that approximately 70 percent of turbine losses are associated with wall and blade boundary layers.

An investigation was made at design Reynolds number for determining the probable error of a single observation for measured variables and calculated quantities, with results from a 16 data point set indicating that the probable errors in total and static efficiencies were ±0.009 and ±0.008, respectively and that probable error is inversely proportional to Reynolds number.

The version with readability index 29 (below) is thoroughly understandable, dignified, courteous, and short. It says exactly the same thing as the version above; there has been not even the slightest change or sacrifice of content:

A radial-flow turbine with a 6.02-inch tip diameter was tested at inlet total pressures from 1.2 to 9.4 pounds per square inch absolute. Corresponding Reynolds numbers ranged from 20,000 to 225,000. The working fluid was argon. (Reynolds number = weight flow ÷ product of viscosity and rotor tip radius, with viscosity measured at turbine entrance conditions.)

Efficiency and equivalent weight flow increased as inlet-pressure and Reynolds number increased. At design equivalent speed and pressure ratio, total efficiency increased from 0.85 to 0.90 with increasing Reynolds number. Static efficiency increased from 0.80 to 0.84. Equivalent weight flow increased about 2 percent. There was some relationship between efficiency and Reynolds number. It showed that about 70 percent of turbine losses are wall and blade boundary layer losses.

Probable error in total efficiency, at design Reynolds number, was calculated to be ±0.009, using a 16 data point set. In static efficiency this was ±0.008. Probable error increased proportionately as Reynolds number decreased.

Writing in the hard-to-understand style of the first version is impossible to justify when the author can make the information as easy to read as the rewritten passage—and with so little effort! How many textbooks have we all read (or tried to read) that were written in a style similar to the first version of that report? Were the *ideas* the learning barrier, or was the writing style?

Always keep in mind: The more difficult your ideas, the more your reader should use his or her energy on *them,* not on your words and sentences.

On Official Tone

Business men and women often feel they must write in a complicated style because they are expected to sound *official.* "After all," they reason, "it's official business, so it should sound like it." Should it? Maybe. But does *tone* make writing official, or does *content?*

Certainly your writing is official whenever its content is the business you are authorized by your employer to conduct on its behalf. But many people try to sound authoritative through writing style alone; they try to sound cold and impersonal. And in the process their writing ends up unclear, sometimes even menacing in tone.

Clarity, courtesy, and official content are the ideal combination for letters and reports of all kinds. Whether your writing is fully official, fully authoritative, has nothing to do with whether it bristles with formality or sounds clear and courteous.

Here is a sample of writing typical of that artificial image of authority writers sometimes try to achieve through tone. You have surely seen writing like this:

. . . the policy of the government to aid in the expansion of small businesses.

The duly executed forms should be submitted to the undersigned upon completion.

Yours truly,

B. L. Cruicci
Applications Officer

Here is the same thing again, this time in clear, courteous language. If the first version was official, this one must be too, because both say the same thing:

. . . the government's policy to help small businesses expand.

Please return the signed forms to me when you have completed them.

Yours truly,

B. L. Cruicci
Applications Officer

On Legal Writing

Another habit that makes writing harder than necessary to understand is the use of legal tone, even when it is not needed. Misguided writers often try to impress readers—to make their writing sound more important than it really is—by trying to imitate legal style. (Robert Gunning, a crusader for plain English in the mid-20th century and an innovator in measuring readability, brought smiles to legions of people who write, with his suggestion: "Write to *express,* not to *impress.*"*

Stereotype legal vocabulary is easy to imitate, with words or phrases such as *herein, with regard to,* or *accordingly* sprinkled among your sentences. The law does have some hard-to-understand but necessary terms of its own, just as medical or scientific writing has. These terms are like a foreign language to others, but they are the working vocabulary of the professional men and women who use them every day. They are the shorthand of the profession; they are not intended for ordinary readers. Lawyers call them "terms of art."

The trouble is, some legal terms can be dangerously deceptive to ordinary readers because they mean something quite different from what we think they should mean. *Quiet enjoyment,* for example, has nothing to do with either quiet or enjoyment. It is a term of property law, going back to Anglo-Saxon law in the 15th and 16th centuries; it means *uninterrupted occupancy.* And, when a trial or hearing is *continued* to a future date, it is actually *discontinued* until that date.

Lawyers often argue that they must use legal terms to say things legally. But many prominent legal authorities, past and present, have argued in rebuttal that plain English is just as legal if it says the right things.

Vocabulary, however, is not the major problem with most legal writing. By far the greater trouble is sentence structure. A popular belief throughout the legal profession holds that periods create loopholes—that a qualifying statement must be in the same sentence as the one it qualifies. Therefore, to avoid loopholes lawyers are trained to avoid periods. This advice is at best questionable, and at worst dangerous. It can cause unbelievably long sentences—often a whole paragraph in length. They may be legally and grammatically correct, but they are sometimes impossible to understand and often cause court battles to determine the real meaning of a document containing them. They fail to communicate. In fact, they hinder communication, as in this example:

> Pursuant to the provisions of the Act, the employer is duly responsible for notification of subsequent revisions in the location of said employer's place of business, subject to termination of exemption in the event of failure to provide such notification.

This means:

> The law requires that your company notify us if it changes its address. If it doesn't notify us, you may lose your exemption.

**The Technique of Clear Writing,* Robert Gunning, McGraw Hill, publisher.

Even lawyers can write clearly and should. Judges beg them to do so. More important, if you are not a lawyer you cannot in any way justify imitating legal style—unless you are trying deliberately to intimidate your reader.

The writer who tries this legal style usually finds it is easy to achieve, on any subject. But it will not impress. It will succeed only in making your writing harder than necessary to read and understand.

In the mid-1970's the state of New York passed a law, the first of its kind, requiring consumer documents and contracts in plain English. About half of the states have passed similar laws, and even where it is not required, companies have learned that plain English is good business.

On Scientific Writing

The problems legal writing can create are also brought about in writing on scientific subjects, by unnecessary use of scientific tone. Some writers try to endow their ideas with more respect than they deserve by expressing them in complex scientific language—even when it is not necessary. People in the so-called "human sciences"—educators, psychologists, and sociologists—seem notorious for this, but they are by no means the only ones. This example is from a doctoral dissertation, published in a professional journal:

. . . Milwaukee: The National Learning Conference, 1989), pp. 207–211.

Integration of aural and visual stimulae produces a more intensified effect in the brain than those resulting from either modality's acting as a single class or type of stimulus.

It is suspected that the same or similar rationale lies behind both the practical and theoretical application. . . .

Here is what that really means:

. . . Milwaukee: The National Learning Conference, 1989), pp. 207–211.

People learn better by hearing and seeing the ideas than by either one alone.

We suspect that the same or similar rationale lies behind both the practical and theoretical application. . . .

But wait. Isn't that information rather commonplace? Is it worth presenting to an audience of professional men and women? Would it have been published if the author had presented it in the plain English of the bottom version?

Notice, incidentally, in the original passage the writer tried to use words more difficult than necessary and lost control: *stimulae* should be *stimuli.* An ironic lesson is revealed here: When writers try to impress readers by straining beyond the limit of their skills, they risk embarrassing themselves instead.

All of which prompts us to conclude: **Scientific vocabulary is a poor substitute for useful information, or for scientific objectivity.** Which in turn takes us back to our opening premise: **The necessary ingredients of good writing are *valuable information* and *clear expression*, and neither is very useful without the other.**

DEVIL'S ADVOCATE: How well can any formula analyze the overall quality of a piece of writing? Let's be reasonable; there are so many things that are unmeasurable.

GURU: Of course there are, and no linguist ever claimed total accuracy. Let's say this about the formula in this chapter. (It would probably be true of any readability formula. There are many of them, and most are more complicated.) A favorable readability index is no assurance of good writing. But an unfavorable one is a strong signal that something is seriously wrong with the writer's word skill or sentence skill. And that "something" will have a direct bearing on the writer's success as a communicator. Shouldn't writers—especially those who are just developing style—want to know that?

Even with its limitations, the fever thermometer is still the medical profession's first diagnostic tool.

DEVIL'S ADVOCATE: Numbers are sometimes an important part of a report or letter. In measuring readability, are they counted as easy words or polysyllables?

GURU: Now you're trying to be more precise than we can be with these measuring instruments. Another comparison might be that a readability formula is more like a yardstick than a micrometer. Yardsticks can't measure in thousandths of an inch, but sometimes—maybe even most of the time—we don't need that kind of precision. If you want to be that analytical, however, here's a sensible way of measuring numbers: Count round numbers (any digit followed only by zeros) as easy; also count any number of four digits or less as easy. The last easy number, then, is 9,999; the first polysyllable number is 10,001 (because 10,000 is a round number).

DEVIL'S ADVOCATE: What's the readability index of: "*Slow but fast telephone poles as to opposed soluble children imitating. Therefore neither hundreds of them and kissing my sister while he flies melting New York, and tomorrow square baseballs minus plus five electric Elvis's Presley monopolies. Even green slow even green melting, but hiring which toothbrushes last year will do it again*"?

GURU: Oh, come now. Are you going to say its readability index is 29 and, therefore, readability formulas prove nothing? In fact, some opponents of readability formulas do make that point, that way. But in the world I live in, people don't write that kind of nonsense. Real people write real things, and they welcome reliable, easy ways of knowing how well they do. Even if the answers are only approximate, they're still remarkably useful.

CHAPTER 5

REVIEW

How alert were you? All of these important points were discussed in the presentation you just read. You should be able to answer them all. If you cannot, you are urged to look them up.

Describe briefly how the reader must divide his or her energy while reading.

____

____

How does the writer influence the reader's ability to understand?

____

____

Please complete this important sentence: The more ______________ *the ideas, the* ______________ *should be the* ______________.

List the three steps in figuring the readability index.

____

____

____

What should be the readability index range for ideal writing? ______________

What is the highest acceptable index? ______________ *The lowest?* ______________

What is the danger if the index is too low?

____

____

In addition to measuring readability, how can the readability index help you analytically to improve your writing?

____

____

What warning must writers keep in mind when using ***any*** *readability formula?*

____

____

Scientific ______________________ *is a shabby substitute for scientific* ______________________.

PRACTICE
Measuring Readability

CHAPTER 5
EXERCISES

Exercise 19.

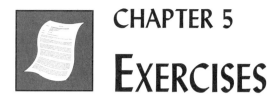

Figure the Readability Index of these two passages:

> *However, it is now our considered opinion that in the light of recurring labor problems in the Brooklyn area, in contrast with a very satisfactory posture of labor in the Staten Island section of the port, and with the presence of the Verazanno Bridge—which has largely eliminated the time element that heretofore was enjoyed by piers in the Brooklyn area—we should make a decision henceforth to discharge all inward cargoes at Piers 19 and 20, Staten Island, until such time as it is demonstrated that the service in Staten Island to shippers is not at least the equivalent of that which has been provided in the Brooklyn area.*

words per sentence: ______

+ percent polysyllables: ______

Readability Index: ______

> *Tungsten can be sintered to high densities at low temperatures if it is alloyed with elements such as nickel. However, an insoluble grain boundary phase makes such alloys weak at high temperatures. This work shows that these alloys are strong if certain third elements, such as copper, are added. The third element makes the nickel soluble in tungsten during sintering. The result is a dense, single-phase alloy that is strong at high temperatures. It can be rolled using standard techniques. The technique of producing precision parts of such alloys was developed by metallurgists at the National Aeronautics and Space Administration.*

words per sentence: ______

+ percent polysyllables: ______

Readability Index: ______

“Thanks to words, we have been able to rise above the brutes. . . .”

—Aldous Huxley

CHAPTER 6

GUIDELINES FOR NONSEXIST WRITING

In our lifetimes, the English language has undergone one of those major, sudden changes that happen only rarely: new words and phrases to remove sexual bias in writing and speech. Interestingly, the United States has led the way in this change and, more specifically, the American business community. In the mid-20th century, American Telephone & Telegraph Company was the world's largest employer of women. It undertook a major program in the 1970's to rewrite all of its corporate documents—personnel forms, instruction manuals, computer letters, and the host of other written pieces that are part of the daily routine of a large and complex organization—to remove all traces of statements that would (and often did) give men career advantages over women. Other companies also led the way, as did most government agencies. The issue drew a great deal of attention, but today we wonder what the fuss was about.

Avoiding sexist language is not only morally correct, doing so is easy. In some writing, it's also the law.

English is notoriously sexist—more so than any other major language, according to language scholars. Still, it is possible to write **anything** without sexist references of any kind. Furthermore, doing so need not create the least bit of awkward wording. Nonsexist language can, and should, appear (also sound) so natural that no one is likely to notice you have said anything differently.

The Infamous Generic *He*

This is, of course, the most common abuse. For years business people (men *and* women) have written statements like: *The customer may not be aware he has this choice.* (Oddly, that usage was the preferred style even when the customer was almost certain to be a woman.) Unthinkable today. So we experimented with ways like: *The customer may not be aware he/she has this choice.* At least, it would avoid complaints. But this phrasing is awkward. The mind's ear cannot hear a slash; the style calls attention to itself, especially if we do it often. *He or she* is slightly better.

One simple change will get rid of three-quarters of the most common sexist references graciously. *He* and *she* are **third person** pronouns. English simply does not have gender-free personal pronouns for third person—in the singular. Switch, then, to plural: *Customers may not be aware they have this choice.* Or, switch to second person: *You may not be aware* . . . (Thoughtful writers try to give instructions using second person pronouns anyhow, where they fit; then the writing addresses the reader directly. The tone becomes warmer and more direct—both desirable traits.)

Switching to the plural will usually work, but not always. For example, in a company memo to all supervisors you might write: *The supervisor must inform an employee, as soon as he or she is suspected of drug abuse, that he or she may face disciplinary action.* A bit like lumpy mashed potatoes; too many *little oddities.* Good writing should not call attention to itself. Second person (*inform you* . . . *that you may face*) won't work here because the writing is addressed to the supervisor, not the suspected employee. Plural (*inform employees* . . . *that they may face*) will not work when the writer wants to refer specifically to one person. So the only available choice is *he or she*—even if the sentence requires it twice, as here. This usage becomes annoying only if you use it repeatedly.

Other *Man* Words

With equal ease you can get rid of all other *man* words. They are never, never necessary. *Man is a social animal* . . . would be better as: *People are social animals.* Anthropologically, both statements say exactly the same thing. *Since the beginning of mankind* . . . would be better as: *Since earliest human history.* . . . In both cases, the nonsexist version is clear, gracious, and just as accurate.

Job Descriptions

They are one of the curses of anybody who has ever tried to write them, and they are a bit harder to keep nonsexist than ordinary text, but still not very hard. Here, more than in most other kinds of writing, old-fashioned (sexist) language habits are an invitation to legal difficulties. Federal courts have ruled that policy statements that refer only to males, even though unintentional, are discriminatory, and some companies have been hurt by resulting law suits.

The problem unique to job descriptions is that often the writer is listing a series of required skills or duties (or both) for *any* employee (male or female) who holds or will hold that job, and each sentence tends to have a pronoun (traditionally *he* in the past) as its subject: *The (job title) must be capable of reading and understanding blueprints according to NA level 6 specifications. He must be capable of making bookkeeping entries and preparing financial statements following NCPA format. He is expected to. . . . He must. . . .* Unacceptable. A statement of that kind would invite Equal Employment Opportunity grievances. *You* or *they* will not work here. Using *he or she* each time would quickly become distracting, and the style awkward. A slightly better way: Combining several statements into fewer longer sentences would mean fewer subjects, therefore fewer sexist/nonsexist pronoun choices. But such sentences quickly become too long and complex to follow, especially for an inexperienced employee (the probable reader).

Solution: Write each section of a job description as a series of phrases, without subjects. This can be done in correct grammar and in smooth, gracious style.

For each section, an introductory phrase contains the subject and main verb; this is followed by a series of sentence fragments, each without a subject, each telling one of the requirements. **Example:**

The (job title) must be capable of:

- reading and understanding blueprints according to NA level 6 specifications.
- making bookkeeping entries and preparing financial statements in NCPA format.
- answering . . .

Be sure to list the ideas vertically, indented, as they are here. This way they can be read separately, rather than as one unbearably long sentence, even though grammatically they are still one sentence. Changes of this kind are easy and will avoid Equal Employment Opportunity grievances. Caution: this format can tend to sound choppy and fragmented; therefore, take extra care to be smooth.

Male Bosses and Female Secretaries?

That may indeed be the situation in many offices, but you must not portray it that way in your writing. You lose no effectiveness whatever by writing, *Every branch manager must be aware of his or her responsibilities. . . .* Or, of course: *Every secretary must be aware of his or her. . . .* Note that the National Council for Teachers of English (NCTE) recommends . . . *must be aware of* ***their****. . . .* That is incorrect grammar, however (singular noun, plural pronoun), and unnecessary. Once poor grammar is endorsed for special situations, where does it stop? Who decides if a situation is special enough? Such permissiveness is an invitation to the "anything goes" attitude in language usage.

Avoid job titles that identify sex. *Mailmen* have become mail *carriers. Salesmen* are *sales representatives. Foremen* are *supervisors.* Airplanes no longer have *stewardesses* but *flight attendants.* Likewise, if you are seriously interested in finding nonsexist descriptions in your writing, you surely can without much effort.

What about *chairman?* No mystery. The *chairman of the board* is now a *chief executive officer.* For lesser ones, use *chairman* for males, *chairwoman* for females. If it is a theoretical one, use *presiding officer,* or *committee head,* or even *person in charge.* Please do **not** use the grossly distasteful *chair.*

Another nonsexist change: Never refer to a grown woman as a *girl.* "*The girl who took the order . . .*" will get you icy stares, and should. "*The woman who took the order . . .*" is just as easy and far more thoughtful. Use *girl* only if she is under 16 years of age.

Thoughtful writers should also be aware that many women dislike being called *ladies.* Men often use *lady* as an intended compliment, but women who are uncomfortable with this point out that the usage is judgmental, that a man does not have the right to decide whether a woman meets his standards of approval, and if men will just call women *women* everyone will be satisfied.

About Ms.

Yes, you should use it in addressing all women—single or married. We do not have different forms of *Mr.* for single and married men. According to surveys, the word *Ms.* (pronounced *mizz*) has slowly but consistently gained in popularity. By the late 1970's, most professional women favored it, and most publishers' style manuals endorsed it. (*The United States Government Printing Office Style Manual,* however, has stayed mum on this subject. *The Chicago Manual of Style* acknowledges the use of *Ms.* but does not encourage or discourage its use.)

DEVIL'S ADVOCATE: Clarify the point, please, about English not having neutral third person pronouns.

GURU: *I* is **first person** (so are *me* and *my*); *you* is **second person.** *He, she,* and *it* are **third person,** and now we're in a bit of trouble; we don't have gender-free versions. Actually, English does give us a neutral third person singular pronoun. It's *one,* but it is rarely used and, therefore, not acceptable. (*The customer may not be aware one has this choice.*) English also allows us *it* for the third person, but that can't be used for people. *They* works nicely for people and things; this is why fellows in good standing of the National Association of Gurus (NAG) recommend switching to the plural to avoid many problems of sexist language. Don't mess with us.

A Georgetown University linguist once proposed *ne* as a compromise to replace both *he* and *she* (because N is positioned in the alphabet half way between H and S). The world wasn't ready for that, however.

DEVIL'S ADVOCATE: But these new phrases sound klutzy.

GURU: They may at first, to some people. But overwhelmingly the public has accepted them with little or no controversy. The public, then, apparently feels that *flight attendant* and *supervisor* are perfectly fine substitutes for *stewardess* and *foreman;* most people don't even notice such changes. But *ne* didn't make it—and won't.

DEVIL'S ADVOCATE: What about a disclaimer at the beginning of a piece of writing, some sort of formal declaration that all male references apply equally to men and women?

GURU: Nope. That won't do. It may have been acceptable when Dr. Benjamin Spock was writing books about raising babies, but not today.

CHAPTER 6

REVIEW

Why are terms like representative *(for* salesman*) or* mail carrier *(for* mailman*) acceptable to readers, while* he/she *and* spokesperson *are not?*

___

___

What is the easiest way to avoid using he *to refer to both men and women?*

___

What is the easiest way to avoid implying that the boss is male and the secretary is female, or the doctor is male and the nurse is female?

___

How can you avoid the awkward usage chair *without being sexist?*

___

What is wrong with a sentence like: "Every parent needs to be aware of this danger to their child."?

___

___

How should you reword the above sentence?

___

___

When is the word gentlemen *appropriate?*

___

How alert were you? All of these important questions were discussed in the chapter you just read. You should be able to answer them all. If you cannot, it's in your interest to look them up.

PRACTICE

Standard English Is Nonsexist.

CHAPTER 6

EXERCISES

Exercise 20.

Rewrite each of the following sentences to eliminate sexist references, yet keeping the style as gracious as possible:

Your Rewrites

Special programs for the wives of attending doctors have been scheduled for Tuesday and Thursday afternoons.

____

____

In recognition of the airline's 50th anniversary, stewardesses will wear gold-trimmed blouses and skirts the week of January 20.

____

____

Why would anyone want to be a fireman?

____

Holly Church, the mayor's wife and a professor of cultural anthropology, will head the multinational committee.

____

____

Every fork truck operator must have his new BDD certification on file by June 30.

____

____

Congressman Rebecca Snavely, chair of the House Education Committee, opposes the Senate plan.

____

____

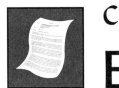

EXERCISE 20 Your rewrites (continued):

When a new employee joins our department, it is everybody's duty to help them and treat them with respect.

One of our service men will be there within an hour.

When you enter the lobby, tell the girl at the security desk you're there to pick up Dr. Miller's report.

A successful man who doesn't perform some community service is not really successful.

Recommended

PRACTICE

Nonsexist English is easy and can sound natural.

Exercise 21.

Usually you can avoid sexist references by switching to the plural, changing *he* to *they, him* to *them, his* to *their.* But that doesn't always work. Sometimes you can avoid needing any pronoun at all, by slight rewording of the phrase containing it. Other times, you may find that *he or she* is just right.

The passage below is thoughtful and courteous—to men. A few word changes in each sentence will make the whole passage nonsexist:

> *Invite the new employee to contribute his talent to the department's daily operations. Encourage him to come to you if he has any questions. Every new employee should be made to feel that his contribution is important to the company.*

Your Rewrite

Recommended

Exercise 22.

Nonsexist language may require a new way of choosing words—especially if you're male. But it is always possible if you are willing. Furthermore, nonsexist language does not require any extra work. A few slight changes to this male-oriented (but otherwise charming) social commentary will make it acceptable to everyone:

> *As he progressed from caveman to nuclear warrior, man's needs became more complex. Animal skins were once adequate body covering; now he needs business suits, jeans, and tuxedos. Campfire rituals were once adequate recreation; now he invents football. Once, a father needed to provide only food and protection. Occasionally, contemplating those earlier times, the chairman of the board can be forgiven for pausing to wonder: Am I any happier than that caveman?*

PRACTICE

Equal treatment of the sexes can add dignity.

Your Rewrite

Recommended

"Words are like leaves; and where they most abound, much fruit of sense beneath is rarely found."

—ALEXANDER POPE

Before You Begin Part 2 . . .

The attitudes and habits we develop in our lifetime are part of whatever forms each of us as a unique being, and changing them is not easy. Our styles of expression, in particular, are habits that mark us; they identify us to those who know us and make a statement about us to strangers observing us for the first time.

If you feel confident of the principles discussed in Part 1—and comfortable with them in your own style of expression, your language usage probably creates clear and readable writing. But if you are experiencing some amount of trouble applying these techniques, or if you are a bit uncomfortable with them, there is no need for concern. Not yet, anyhow. We often need practice to break old habits. As long as you need to stop and think about the Six Principles of Clear Writing and deliberately force yourself to make changes, you may be writing more slowly than before. But nothing about these principles is very difficult, except changing those earlier habits. Once you can apply the six principles without having to remind yourself of them and without deliberately forcing yourself, you should gain the clarity of style, and the speed, that accomplished writers enjoy.

"To produce a mighty book you must choose a mighty theme."

—HERMAN MELVILLE

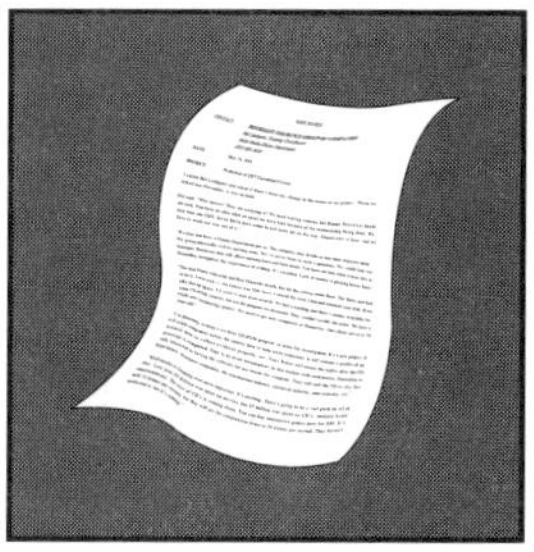

Part 2
On Organizing

Power to the Reader

- Learning Power
- The Inverted Pyramid Structure
- The Five W's of Journalism
- A Recommended Format for Formal Reports
- A Checklist for Organizing

Sense and Nonsense about Planning (Pre-Writing)

- How to Outsmart the Deadline
- The Importance of the False Start
- Mapping the Trip
- The Real Way to Outline

Finishing Touches of the Pros

- Headings: Readers Love Them
- The Importance of White Space
- Paragraph Structuring
- Where Should Graphics Go?
- Ways to Add Emphasis
- Fact and Fancy about Letters
- About Dictation

Reviewing and Editing the Writing of Others

What Computers Can and Can't Do for Writers

CHAPTER 7

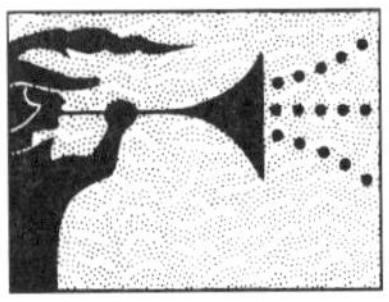

POWER TO THE READER

> The principles of clarity discussed in Part 1 are useful for all kinds of writing—whether a great novel, a newspaper article, or a report of any kind. The advice in Part 2, however, applies only to that kind of writing we call *expository*.

All writing (except poetry and holy Scripture) is divided into two categories: expository and narrative. It is expository if its purpose is purely to convey information—either to inform or to persuade. All business writing and most newspaper writing is expository. Add one more ingredient, plot, and the writing becomes *narrative*. Now the reader reads not only for the information, but also for the interesting way the writer assembles and presents it—the story line. We repeat: The principles of organizing presented here are most useful for expository writing. In fact, they would almost certainly hinder your ability to develop an artistic or exciting plot.

Every writer puts words on paper for a *reader*, and the successful writer *becomes* successful by understanding and concentrating on readers' needs. In organizing, even more than in choosing words and combining them into sentences, the writer/sender can greatly help—or hinder—the reader/receiver's ability to receive. And if you don't help, you will almost certainly hinder. Empowerment is yours, writer, to be passed on to your reader. With the same principle of organizing expository information (and there is basically only one), you can empower virtually every kind of reader—the one who wishes to plunge into your work and study every word carefully, or the one who needs only the most important points and wants then to go to something else quickly, or the reader in between, who will decide while reading how deeply to examine your information. With one principle, you can empower all three to read efficiently, each satisfying his or her own needs, and to understand and retain.

And that principle is: **Start with your conclusion, then spend the rest of the writing supporting it.**

Learning Power

How predictable expository readers are! We know that they usually read for information, not for pleasure, and that other demands compete for their time—especially in the world of work. We know, too, that first impressions will strongly influence most readers' attitudes as they receive the rest. You win or lose your reader early. In organizing, then, *the thoughtful writer tries to convey as much information as possible, as accurately and clearly as possible, and—yes—in as little reading as possible.* Quite a noble goal.

Compare a cracking good mystery story (narrative form) with a newspaper account of the same events (expository form). If the mystery novelist is skillful enough, readers quickly become so enthralled they are trapped into the ". . . I couldn't put it down" mood. We don't want to put it down, and if someone tells us how it ends, that mood is broken. That person who told us how it ends has interfered with the writer's creative skill and artistry as a weaver of plot, and with our right to enjoy it.

But in the newspaper report of those same events the reader is reading just for the information, not for the enjoyment of following a plot as it unfolds. Now, the *how it ends* information, unwelcomed in the storyteller's version if it came too early, is the most important thing the reader wants to know. Did Congress vote yes or no? Who won the game last night? Get to the point fast. Often the *headline* is all readers need.

And so, whereas narrative readers ". . . can't put it down," expository readers are eager to put it down as soon as they feel they have read all they need.

Now comes the danger: Your reader may put it down too soon. He or she may quickly scan a report or memorandum and decide (wrongly) *"This doesn't contain information I need."* Or, he or she may read some important information, be pleased, then say (again wrongly) *"Okay, good stuff. I don't need the rest,"* and miss something even more important. How can readers decide accurately when to stop, unless in retrospect, after reading the whole thing? Writers must help them. The skillful writer wants—needs—to ensure that his or her *important* information is received properly. What's really important? What is the one statement about which you would be willing to say: *"It's all right if my reader reads nothing else"*? That information should be at the beginning. If it is, it's truly all right if the reader reads nothing else. Again, the skillful writer tries to convey as much information as possible, as accurately and clearly as possible, in as little reading as possible. You have empowered your reader when you have succeeded in doing this.

Writers still learning their craft can find valuable lessons about organizing expository writing in a well-written newspaper article. Newspaper and magazine publishers and universities have conducted detailed studies to discover how we read, and these have revealed some things that everyone who writes ought to know about readers of expository information.

In wanting to stop early, the typical reader is not lazy or irresponsible. It's simply that the expository reader is reading only for information. He or she is probably busy and eager to receive important information quickly, then move on. This is especially true if your reader is a top executive.

Start with the conclusion, then spend the rest of the writing supporting it, whether you are writing a business letter or memo, a church or club newsletter, or a complicated engineering or financial report.

Never make readers wonder, *What are you getting at?* Get to the point fast. There are some exceptions, which will be discussed later, but generally it's unwise to build up gradually to your most important information at or near the end.

Again, putting your conclusions *at (or very near) the beginning* satisfies all possible readers. **If your reader wants only the most important information, placing it first guarantees he or she will get what *you* considered most important. Another reader may want every word in detail. Or a third kind of reader might like to read selectively—some passages but not others.** When you write, you can't tell. But by putting your conclusions first, then following with the supporting information, you give any reader the choice.

Narrative (storytelling) structure:

> Experts have been divided since World War II on the important question: Do some dogs have more fleas than other dogs, or fewer fleas? By a slight majority, public opinion favors the *more fleas* theory. Grants from the National Science Foundation sponsored research on this subject at major universities in 1972 and 1993, but even more recent researchers remain divided. The Center for Bugs and Critters (CBC) has just concluded a 5-year research program in search of a definitive answer to this pressing question. A survey form and a kit (for counting fleas) were sent to all dog owners in Canada. Owners of wolves were excluded. The response rate. . . .
>
> 41 pages follow, mostly on the survey methods. THEN:
>
> The results show clearly that, although most people think some dogs have more fleas than other dogs, the opposite is true; analysis of the statistics proves that some dogs have fewer fleas than other dogs. The Société Français des Chiennes concurs with our findings.

Expository (reporting) structure:

> Most people think some dogs have more fleas than other dogs. Actually, the opposite is true; new research by the CBC shows clearly that some dogs have fewer fleas than other dogs.
>
> *Reader reaction 1:* Okay, that's what we needed to know. Thanks.
>
> *Reader reaction 2:* That troubles me a little. I need to study all 41 pages of this report carefully.
>
> *Reader reaction 3:* I'm not surprised, but I'll need to take a look closely at the parts on. . . .

Even if your reader intends to read every word in great detail, he or she is a *better* reader having received the conclusion first. Reading experts tell us a summary statement, or *overview,* is important if the reader is to understand—especially for difficult information. Without it, you give the receiving brain isolated bits of information; because nothing ties them together, that receiving brain doesn't know what to do with them until the end. First declare what the brain is going to receive, then those same bits of information are no longer isolated; the reader knows what to do with them. **Armed with that overview, he or she can understand the details better and will retain them longer.**

In truth, this is not a principle of writing but of *learning.* The gifted teacher starts by saying: "*Here's what we're going to do today, here's how we're going to do it, and here's why it's important to you.*" And the student becomes a better learner.

The elevator door statement. Picture this scene. As you step out of the elevator at your office, your boss steps in, and as you pass each other he or she asks, *"What did you decide about the GSA letter?"* You have only the few seconds that elevator door will stay open, while you hold the rubber bumper that keeps it open, to give an intelligent answer. And you always manage to do so. Just before the menacing buzzers and alarm bells go off, you reply, *"It sounds good, but only if they give us the extra time I asked for."* The boss says as the doors close, *"Fax that to them."*

What invaluable communication tools elevator doors are! They force us to organize our thoughts properly, and every writer should have a set at his or her desk. The intimidating mental image of alarm bells and flashing lights forces us to channel our thoughts and identify the one short statement about which we would be willing to say: *"It's all right if I say nothing else."*

But we are intelligent beings. Can we not find ways to think quickly and accurately without threat? Again, at your desk, planning a report, ask yourself: *"What is that statement about which I am willing to say: It's all right if my reader reads nothing else."*? That is your elevator door statement. It is your conclusion, the top of your valuable collection of information. The rest of the report fills in the details.

Or Else: When giving expository information, writers should get to the point quickly for still another reason: If you don't tell in advance what important point (or points) you are trying to make, your reader might arrive at some conclusion other than the one you intended; the results may be disastrous.

Do not let either of those things happen to your important information. The two main goals here are precision and efficiency. This whole idea of opening with the conclusion shifts the burden of communication from the reader to the writer. *You* control what readers get out of your writing by declaring early what they *should* get out of it. Nothing is left to chance.

The Inverted Pyramid Structure

To satisfy the reader's need for the overview at or near the beginning, journalism has given us the *Inverted Pyramid Structure.* That term should be important to your writing the rest of your life. The Inverted Pyramid is the structure that presents the most important information early, then spends the rest of the writing supporting it.

Here is what it looks like in its simplest form:

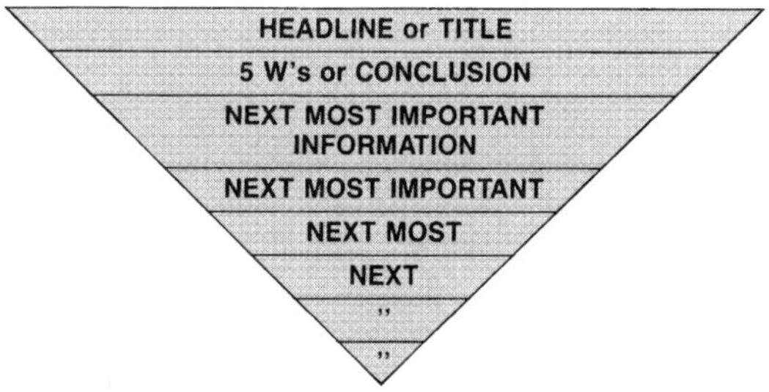

Notice that the simplest Inverted Pyramid is heavy with information at the top and fades into nothingness at the bottom. That is how most newspaper articles are organized, and it is how you should organize all reports and most letters.* Regardless of what name we give the structure, the realistic writer starts with the attitude that the reader may be interested in reading only a small part of the writing, especially if it is a report. Therefore, he or she puts everything the reader **must** learn into the early paragraphs.

The 5 W's of Journalism

To ensure that the writer puts the most important information at the beginning, sages centuries ago created the 5 *W's* of journalism: *Who, What, When, Where, and Why.* These go in the first paragraph. And by so doing they ensure that every reader will receive the most important information describing a news event, even if he or she reads no further. Who, What, When, Where, and Why—though not necessarily in that order.

Your letters and reports may not have all five of the W's. You may have just one—What. More likely, two—*What* and *Why.* That conclusion, or overview statement, is the real reason for the writing.

Here is an example of a report structured as an Inverted Pyramid. First, a good opening paragraph, or overview statement (*What, When,* and *Why*):

A serious and costly packaging problem recently developed in our Virtual Projection Department. To solve it, I recommend we upgrade the Fracklin CC-8511 fulfillment station by adding a digital plotting assembly as soon as possible. On a 5-year lease, this will cost $57,200 ($933.33 per month, which includes installation and service). We estimate the upgrade will reduce shipping and labor costs $78,200 in that period, and it will eliminate the division's only serious source of customer complaints. If possible, I would like to discuss this matter with you before the department's February 19 planning committee meeting.

Then the rest of the report (the details), in order of importance:

The company now manufactures downlink terminal adapters faster than we can ship them. Backups result, and customer complaints forced us to ship 31 special orders by air freight in the fourth quarter, at an average cost of $108.38 per order ($76.00 for the platform and $32.38 for the converter). By comparison, regular United Parcel Service costs $21.72 ($13.86 and $7.86). We were unable to charge the difference ($86.66 per shipment) to the customers because the fault was ours, not theirs. Our extra shipping cost for the quarter (31 shipments at $86.66) was $2,686.

*Although the generally accepted term for this structure in writing is *Inverted Pyramid,* some writers argue that the concept is better described by just the word *Pyramid,* and drawn with the point up. Their thinking: The smallest section (the point), not the largest, should hold the most precious content. But this comparison to the Egyptian pyramids is inaccurate; the pharaoh's chamber was not at the top *or* bottom, but somewhere in between (different places in different pyramids), to be as hard as possible for grave robbers to find. The two versions of the pyramid are equally useful, but *Inverted Pyramid* is the more common term.

To get those orders out on time, a packaging operator worked overtime an average of 4.6 hours per week during the fourth quarter, at $20.47 per hour, or $1,224 for the quarter.

The combined extra expense for the quarter, then, was $3,910. That expense this year will be $15,640, or a total of $78,200 over the next 5 years, if sales volume stays the same and shipping rates and labor costs don't go up.

The Fracklin CC-8511 operates at 4100 CRS, which met our needs when we purchased it two years ago. We knew then that the upgrade would eventually be needed, but the recent Mexican joint venture created the need earlier than we had planned. The upgrade component runs at 5,500 CRS. According to our latest market forecast, that will meet our needs for the next six years.

Fay Simmons has received bids from three companies, and she recommends the Fracklin DPA-2. The manufacturer can deliver and install it within three weeks. We have space for this equipment in the present packaging line area.

Fay saw this problem coming last summer and wrote to Tom Shields on August 20, but no action was taken.

That report gave power to the reader. Imagine if it had begun:

On August 20 Fay Simmons wrote a memo to Tom Shields and recommended . . .

. . . then built to the conclusion last, including the request to meet before February 19. A SOBERING THOUGHT: Might Fay Simmons indeed have written her August 20 memo structured that way? Might this be the reason the department now faces a loss of $78,200 if something isn't done?

Why write the rest? You may ask, "*If the reader gets all the significant information in only a fraction of the writing, why go through all the trouble of writing pages and pages of support?*" You write the rest to clarify to the reader how you arrived at those key points in the overview statement, just in case he or she wants that information. Your reader may choose to read the entire report, beginning to end, or just the overview statement. The writer never knows, and any reader is entitled to that choice. But even if his or her choice is to read only the overview information, any reader is comforted by the presence of that supporting documentation. It is the backup information; its presence ensures that what you said up front is correct. Take away that supporting documentation, and he or she may not trust that important information in the overview.

Structuring the rest. Once you have written the overview, there are basically three ways you can organize the rest of the information that makes up the whole Inverted Pyramid:

- in order of importance (usually most desirable for most readers)
- in logical order
- in chronological order

(There is a fourth way: **Chaos.** And if it is not one of the first three, it will surely be number four; thoughtful readers call this *the mind dump,* and resent it.)

Here is an example of the beginning of a letter organized as an Inverted Pyramid. It gets to the point fast:

Ms. Falberg,

As you requested, we have thoroughly examined the operations of Maryland Environmental Enterprise, Inc.'s Greenhouse Division. We found no serious weaknesses.

A few of your practices we feel are inefficient. We have listed these by department, along with detailed suggestions for improvement. All of these suggested changes can be made with your existing staff, but a few will require new equipment. In all cases, the savings brought about by the change will pay for the new equipment in less than a year. May I stress, however, that these are all minor suggestions . . .

Notice that the writer gives the summary or conclusion in the first paragraph. The reader learns immediately that the writer found no serious weaknesses. Then, quickly, the reader also learns the next most important information: that the Greenhouse Division has a few inefficient practices, and that detailed explanations follow for each department. All of this information is the overview. The rest of the letter, although not shown here, gives the details (for the reader who chooses to continue). The simplest Inverted Pyramid would discuss the departments one by one. They might be listed in order of importance—or perhaps geographically, or by some other convenient pattern. Each section, incidentally, might be structured as a minor Inverted Pyramid—with its own conclusion at its beginning. Many variations are possible for the details, but they all have one thing in common: They are unified by a strong opening statement.

If the reader (Ms. Falberg) decides she has learned all she needs to know, she might forward the letter on to a subordinate who is responsible for the details. Again, power—quick power—to the reader. A gift from the writer.

How to end: There is no need for a summary or wrap-up statement at the end. Writers like to end dramatically; readers don't care. In fact, a proper Inverted Pyramid encourages most readers to stop early, by making it easy to do so reliably. Therefore, most readers will never know how you ended. **The best advice on how to end seems to be: WHEN YOU HAVE NOTHING MORE TO SAY, JUST STOP.** This is the opposite of the advice recommended for public speaking. If you have studied public speaking, you probably learned: *Tell them what you're going to say; then say it; then tell them what you have said.* Ending with a fanfare is an excellent guide for a speech; it builds drama at the end and puts audiences in the mood to applaud. But in writing, don't feel you must use a dramatic ending. Many of the best writers—newspaper columnists for example—usually don't use it. Remember, if the expository *writer* is skillful the *reader* may not—often need not—be around at the end. Your best and most important reader probably won't know, or care, what was in the third paragraph of the second last page. Again: When you have nothing more to say, just stop.

Two NEVER-NEVER rules for placing important information. (1) If you feel the need to end with a fanfare, (speakers like this technique because the dramatic ending generates applause), follow the public speaking advice: Repeat the conclusion, or overview statement, at the end. Speakers like this technique because the dramatic ending puts audiences in the mood to applaud. Thoughtful writers must never, never, however, set aside some important *new* information for a dramatic ending! Think, now. The Inverted Pyramid structure, with its most important information up front and followed by supporting information, encourages thoughtful readers to stop when they have had enough. Or rather, when they *think* they have had enough. Encouraging (or tempting) readers to stop early, then presenting important information at the end, is not a very prudent thing to do.

(2) If for some thoughtful reason you sense danger in presenting your conclusion at the beginning of a report, the second most useful place is at the end. Never, never, however, place it anywhere in between! Lacking that summary statement up front, wise readers might turn to the end for it; they have learned that's where untrained writers often lay their pot of gold to rest. But if it isn't at the beginning or end, few readers will be motivated to explore a third location in search of the information that would help them the most, or that you most want them to receive. Some may be motivated enough to read on anyhow, but they will be disadvantaged readers; they will lack the one piece of information that makes all the pieces fall in place.

Inexperienced writers often resist the idea of the Inverted Pyramid. They're likely to express two common objections: **First, putting the conclusion at the beginning is the opposite of most people's natural tendency.** To do so requires reversing the order of our thinking. For lack of better guidance, writers often tend to tell things in the order they lived them. You are then writing a diary, not a report, or a children's story beginning, "Once upon a time. . . ." Usually there is little relationship between the order you learned your information and the order in which your reader should learn it. If your thinking was open-minded, you gathered the supporting information first, then examined it, then arrived at the conclusions and recommendations last. In writing the report, using your memory as a guide is easy, but the most important information usually ends up at the end, setting up an awkward flow of information for the reader. (But better than if the overview statement is buried somewhere in the middle.)

Second, writers often resist the Inverted Pyramid because their pride is hurt by the thought that the reader may not read every word. This is especially true if the writer has done a good job, and knows it, and the reader is his or her manager. This proud worker wants every reader to study every word from beginning to end; we all want our good work to be recognized. But it is unreasonable to expect a reader to read for the purpose of admiring what a good job we did. In fact, a far higher professional compliment comes when managers say: "Just tell me your conclusions. I don't need to know the details because I know how good you are, and I trust your work is reliable and accurate." Prudent managers want employees that good, and nurture them, and place a high value on their ability to think clearly and write clearly.

A Comparison of Structures: If the conclusion of an expository piece isn't at the beginning, the next best place (but not very good) is the end; careful readers often hunt for it there. It may be somewhere in between, however. And if it is, will readers search for it? Will they know it when they see it?

But there can be something more damaging even than an overview statement buried somewhere in the middle, and that is: Several important statements, which together make up the writer's overview, scattered in different locations.

The humorous essay below suffers from that affliction. It may not be a major error here, because the piece is written more to entertain than to inform. But with a little reorganizing, the information could do both equally well. After reading it, can you identify the three important pieces of advice and rewrite the essay in the expository (Inverted Pyramid) form, with the overview statement up front?

HOW TO EAT A CORNED BEEF SANDWICH

My friend Freddy knows corned beef. He is the Midwest America corned beef maven of mavens, and he doesn't mind sharing his knowledge with others. Doesn't mind? He considers this to be his ministry; it is his contribution to improving the planet. In fact, you can't shut him up on the subject. In fact, he has been known to approach strangers and begin soliloquizing on the subject. Once a small woman, terrified, gave him a dollar to go away. His wife, Judy, located her and gave it back.

From his Dos Lagos headquarters, this pioneer has tried to influence the restaurant profession on behalf of corned beef sandwich aficionados everywhere, but some delicatessen owners petitioned city hall, and the police took away his license to conduct public seminars, which nobody attended anyhow, even though they were free.

One challenge that confronts you, Freddy warns, is the corned beef meatball. I happen to agree. You ordered a sandwich, but you get this rather large meatball, albeit between two slices of bread. It is the object of your joy, but it resides in the middle, and out there beyond it, stretching to the horizons of your bread—nothing.

You are permitted, when confronted with this alarming state of affairs, to take vigilante action. In polite company, in fact, you would be expected to disassemble the defective product, redistribute its assets, then reassemble. A-ah, that's good. At this point you're ready to consider peripherals. Mustard? Yellow, of course—if any. Lettuce and/or tomato? No. Not even served separately; this is not a CBLT. Swiss Cheese? Optional. Mayonnaise? Shame on you; don't confuse corned beef with good ham. And don't bother with corned beef-chopped liver combo. Save some money and just order the chopped liver; it would overpower the more delicate corned beef. Pastrami and chopped liver, maybe.

But the fundamental threat to the sandwich, Freddy pontificates, and again I agree, is too much corned beef. Yes, there can be too much. Restaurants simply try to jam more down our throats than we need, so they can charge more. This is a newly emerged crisis in our society, and it has been allowed to remain unaddressed, and therefore to worsen, because few people understand a good corned beef on rye and a dill pickle any more. People have been conditioned to think bad is good. They think good is when you can't open your mouth wide enough to bite both sides of the bread. Freddy teaches that the corned beef should be, at most, about as thick as one of the slices of bread—certainly no thicker—so you get the sweet balance of both flavors, and if the bread is there just to keep your fingers from getting a little greasy, it's cheaper to ask for the corned beef between two napkins, or take half of it home for another sandwich tomorrow, or an omelet.

How about those yuppies and yuppypersonators who ask for extra lean? Extra lean is the third peril. We'll have none of it. A good deli should refuse to serve it, Freddy believes, and a good counter man who knows bad from good—in customers as well as corned beef—might just as well serve up dried rabbit between two slices of rye, confident the extra lean requesters can't tell the difference and deserve what they get. It is *not* true that any corned beef is better than none. Corned beef is not watermelon, Freddy has warned investigating committees for years.

White bread instead of rye? Okay, the maven of mavens says, but you should use a little less corned beef to preserve the delicate balance of tastes.

Corned beef between potato pancakes? Don't even sit near anyone who orders that; move to another table. Corned beef and cabbage? Two strong thumbs up, but not within Freddy's credentialed area of expertise. He refers CBC inquiries to Northeastern America maven of mavens Sean O'Rourke of Boston.

Quickly now, can you identify the information in that short piece which should be the opening paragraph of an Inverted Pyramid structure—the advice about which the writer would say: "*It's all right if readers read nothing else*"? Freddy's conclusion, or overview statement, comprises* three important pieces of advice. The trouble is, they don't appear together anywhere in the writing. In order of importance:

- too much meat
- the corned beef meatball
- the extra lean sandwich

Here, then, is an appropriate opening paragraph:

Special knowledge is required for full enjoyment of a corned beef sandwich. Freddy, the Midwest America maven of mavens, gives this advice to consumers: (1) Be suspicious of sandwiches containing too much meat. (2) Disassemble and redistribute a sandwich that has all the corned beef piled in the middle like a meatball. (3) Think hard before ordering extra lean; unpleasant things sometimes happen.

Followed by separate sections discussing those three points, including all the colorful comments:

- The fundamental threat to the sandwich, Freddy pontificates, is too much corned beef. Yes, there can be too much. Restaurants simply try to jam. . . .
- Freddy warns of the challenge presented by the corned beef meatball. You ordered a sandwich but get a rather large meatball, albeit between two slices. . . .
- The maven of mavens questions the judgment of yuppies and yuppypersonators who ask for extra lean. He warns that extra lean is the third peril and we should have none of it, and that a good deli should refuse . . .

Now the reader gets the less important information: mustard; no lettuce and/or tomato; swiss cheese; no mayonnaise. Special advice on white bread and confrontations regarding potato pancakes.

Freddy's eccentricities, and his friend's observations on them, might come next. (Some writers might, however, consider these important enough that readers should know of them earlier.)

Nearing the bottom of the Inverted Pyramid, the two strong thumbs up for corned beef and cabbage and Sean O'Rourke.

And last (and least), Freddy lives and operates in Dos Lagos.

***Comprises* is correct. The whole comprises the parts. The U.S. *comprises* 50 states; not *is comprised of* . . .

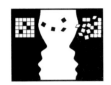

A Recommended Format for Formal Reports

For most reports and letters, a simple Inverted Pyramid structure is usually easy to plan. But the longer the piece, the harder it is to organize. And, of course, it's the long ones that most need to be well organized, in order to help the reader receive and process your information efficiently.

No one format works best for all reports. But you may find the following one useful as a guide, then tailor it to fit your particular body of information.

This recommended structure contains eight basic sections. You may not need them all, especially in a short report; in fact, using all eight would create a very formal document such as an engineering or scientific research report. Here are the eight sections, in the order in which the reader reads them. *But note that you cannot possibly write them in that order; in fact, you must write them in the exact opposite order.* You will understand why as you understand what they contain:

- **Title.** A good title can be immensely useful. Write it carefully. And write it last. *It should be a highly condensed version of the whole report,* and to achieve that goal it should quickly tell the subject and, if possible, the conclusion. But most writers omit the conclusion. Without it, the reader is deprived of the first opportunity to read with power—and the first opportunity to exercise the choice of stopping, satisfied. (The following title doesn't quite fulfill its role: "The Tank as an Instrument of War." A much more informative one: "The Declining Role of the Tank as an Instrument of War.") Limit the title to 120 typewritten characters or less—preferably much less.
- **Abstract.** A capsule version of the whole report. It tells subject, conclusions, and how you arrived at those conclusions. Limit it to 50 to 100 words. The abstract is useful for library files, computerized information retrieval systems, and abstract journals; traditionally, it does not appear in the report. *If you need an abstract, write it only after you have written the body and all the other preliminary sections (except the title). Otherwise, it might not contain the right key words, and future literature searchers might not find your information.*
- **Summary.** This is the most important section of most reports. The summary contains exactly the same information as the abstract—subject, conclusions, and how you arrived at those conclusions—but in more detail. It is the first thing the reader reads after the title, and in many cases the only thing (if it is informative enough). Limit it to 200 to 300 words—to fit on one page if possible. Rarely should it be longer than one page, and certainly no longer than two. Don't worry if the abstract and summary sound much alike; they never appear together.
- **Introduction.** Not to be confused with the summary or abstract. The introduction should give background information—reasons for doing the work you are reporting, possible benefits, a description of past work on the subject, etc. Limit it to one page, or 200 to 300 words.
- **Conclusion.** Think hard here, to say what is really of significance. Don't be misled by the word *conclusion.* This is not the conclusion of the report in the sense of concluding remarks. Rather, it is the conclusion

you reached as a result of the work you are reporting, and that is usually the last thing you learned while doing the work. But it should be the first thing your reader learns. Limit this to 50 to 100 words. If you need more, you probably haven't thought carefully enough: *What is the real meaning of this work I'm reporting?*

- **Recommendations.** This section is optional. Your conclusions may contain your recommendations. Or you may have none. But if you do make recommendations, they should be introduced up front, and you are entitled to state your reasons for them briefly up front—especially if those recommendations may surprise or upset your reader. You will discuss them fully in the main body of the report, but this is where you first announce them and, briefly, explain your reasons for them. Limit this section to one page, or 200 to 300 words.
- **Discussion.** This is the main body of the report. Here the writer discusses his or her work, findings, and reasoning in full detail and in all their glory. If you have done everything else correctly, the body can run hundreds of pages without inconveniencing the reader. If it runs longer than a page or two, however, try to break it into subsections with separate subheadings. (In that case, a table of contents should be included.)
- **Appendixes.** Try not to use them. Put charts, tables, etc. in the body where you discuss them, unless there are too many. If possible, limit appendixes to optional information. (See page 139.)

Notice there is some planned repetition in this recommended format—particularly in the early sections. Each time, however, the reader gets more detail. If you put the proper information into these sections, you are forced to construct an Inverted Pyramid. Your reader gets the choice of reading just a highly condensed version, or the condensed version followed by all the details, or the condensed version followed by just those details he or she chooses to read. What a heavenly joy for readers. *Empowerment.*

But notice too, as we said before, *you cannot possibly WRITE these eight sections in the order they unfold before the reader.* Your reader receives them from top to bottom; **you must write them in the OPPOSITE order—from the bottom of the Inverted Pyramid to the top.** Write the body first, planning it as an overall Inverted Pyramid.* Then write the preliminary sections. Especially, you should write conclusions, summary, abstract, and title last; each one is a progressively more condensed version of the body and, therefore, you cannot possibly write them intelligently until you have written the body. If you write these sections first, you are creating them before you have done the major

*Here is an interesting variation of the Inverted Pyramid structure. If the work that is the subject of your report unfolded in a sequence of events, you may choose to report them that way (*after* the conclusion or overview), in the order they happened. Almost like "*Once upon a time . . .*," the storyteller's structure, with the conclusion at the end. But before reading this, the reader has already read the conclusion; now, as you build back up to it, he or she understands where you're going, and why. We all know this technique as *flashback,* and we enjoy it because it allows a skillful writer to combine the efficiency of the expository form AND artistry of the narrative.

thinking each one requires, and, as a result, they may not accurately reflect the body. This is a common flaw. It is probably the reason so many reports are hard to retrieve later in library searches; they are indexed and filed under the wrong **key words** because the title and abstract may not contain the right ones. Why not? Because so many authors write their titles and abstracts in advance, before they have learned what all the key words will be. Nobody will ever know how much duplicated research this causes—especially in organizations using computerized information retrieval systems. Duplicated because the second researcher didn't find the record of the first work in his or her literature search.

Your report may not need all of these eight sections. Or it may need these plus others. Again, this format is only a guide. It's reasonable to presume, however, that any serious report will have at least a title, summary, and body.

Far more important than following a rigid format, you must understand the reasons behind the Inverted Pyramid theory and why this structure does so much good for so many readers. If you do, you can intelligently design a format for each report to fit the information that particular report contains.

The Inverted Pyramid's One Disadvantage

> Dear Mr. DiMaria,
>
> We're sorry, but our company is unable to deliver your computer-animated graphics display by May 15, as you . . .

(Groan. Slams letter on desk. Gets up and walks a few steps from desk. Pounds forehead.)

DiMaria *(slowly):* Oh, no! How could they do this? We'll miss the Chicago meeting. *(Rage follows. He doesn't read the rest but has already decided he will never do business with that [expletive deleted] company again!)*

Rather, try:

> Dear Mr. DiMaria,
>
> You'll recall you placed your order and instructed us on January 29 to begin construction of your computer-animated graphics display.

DiMaria: Oh, oh. Is something wrong? *He reads on:*

> . . . On March 4 you instructed us to simulate a flight path with fiber optics of various colors, and to add rounded side panels. We were able to make these changes.

DiMaria: I smell trouble. *Then:*

> . . . On April 7, according to our records, Ms. Brunay phoned and instructed us to change the wording. Then, just as we were . . .

DiMaria: I'm not going to like this.

But it's too late. Frank DiMaria already knows that bad news is coming, that he (not the supplier) is the cause, and that the supplier has been cooperative and its representative is trying to deliver the inevitable bad news as graciously as possible.

Sadly, he recalls that the day he ordered the last change the representative told Ms. Brunay delivery might be late, but he just said, "I'm sure they can take care of it."

Few of life's rules are absolute, and the Inverted Pyramid structure does have one disadvantage—sometimes: Putting the conclusion at the beginning does not allow writers to be very subtle; this structure may be too hard-hitting for the presentation of bad news. If the conclusion is likely to upset your reader, telling it first might close his or her mind to the supporting facts. In that case, the thoughtful writer might deliberately choose to write a narrative—hold the conclusion from the beginning and *start with the supporting information*—slowly but inevitably leading to the conclusions or recommendations in such a way that the reader cannot escape them.

Nothing can turn bad news into good news. But the thoughtful writer should try to ease the discomfort for the person at the other end. This is the kind of thing considerate writers try to do. Trying to retain the reader's good will is also good business.

Never lead up to the main point slowly in a *report*, however. You may put an unfavorable conclusion at the end in a *letter* if you wish, because a letter is short and addressed to one person, and you can reasonably assume that person will read the whole thing. But if important information doesn't come very early in a report, your reader may not stay around very long; the carefully planned and clearly written conclusion, or overview statement, should always appear at the beginning.

A Checklist for Organizing

Structure is harder to evaluate than clarity. No one has devised a way to measure numerically whether ideas are arranged in some helpful, orderly sequence. Yet some way of evaluating—some checklist—is helpful.

It is reasonable to expect a few basic things of any piece of expository writing if it is to be well structured. These four questions might make a helpful checklist, especially for reports:

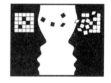

- ✔ Is there a summary or overview statement very early?
- ✔ Is all the information in some helpful sequence?
- ✔ Is the emphasis of the various ideas in proportion to their importance?
- ✔ Are there headings to help the reader?

Is there a full conclusion or overview statement very early? Remember, the reader has the right to choose reading only that, and he or she may not stay around to read very long or work very hard to find it. Remember too, even readers who intend to read every word carefully can understand the details better if they have had the overview first. If you stop and think about it, you'll almost certainly agree that's true of you when you are the reader.

Is all the information in some helpful sequence? The sections may be arranged by order of importance, or (in special cases) events may unfold in chronological order, or data may be listed by company departments or by product. But some method of arranging your information is demanded from beginning to end, and it should be obvious even to a scanning reader.

Is the emphasis of the various ideas in proportion to their importance? Two factors send the reader a subconscious message suggesting how important an idea is, even before it is read: the size of the section, and its location. In the traditional Inverted Pyramid structure, then, the important sections (after the conclusion or overview statement) should normally be longer near the front and get shorter as the bottom of the pyramid narrows.

Are there headings to help the reader? Headings and sub-headings are like road signs, guiding the reader on his or her trip. (See Chapter 9.) No report can be considered well structured without them, especially if it's very long.

WE REPEAT: When structuring your letters or reports, your job is to tell as much as possible, as clearly and accurately as possible, in as little reading as possible. The reader should not need to work harder than necessary to receive and understand your ideas. When is reading harder than necessary? When the writer did not do everything in his or her power to make it easier for the reader. Always the reader. **Everything you do in writing—in both clarity and organizing—is for the benefit of that person at the receiving end. He or she is the only reason you write.**

DEVIL'S ADVOCATE: You compared the narrative form to a children's story, "Once upon a time . . ." or a great mystery, with the conclusion at the end. Obviously, people like to read that way.

GURU: Yes, but only for pleasure. Not when they're reading just for some information they need.

DEVIL'S ADVOCATE: Also, obviously people like to write "*Once upon a time . . .*" stories.

GURU: Well, they need to understand the differing needs of narrative and expository *readers.* Why do inexperienced writers like to tell things in the order they happened? Because it's easier; they use their memories as a guide. But if the reader has to go through all you went through to learn what you learned, what does he or she need you for?

DEVIL'S ADVOCATE: The Inverted Pyramid structure showcases the conclusion. BUT, if the reader gets that first, there's a danger he or she will think I did the work with my mind made up in advance, and then looked for information to support premature conclusions. I risk being perceived as doing biased work. I don't need this.

GURU: Oh, the wisdom of the literary architects who gave us the Inverted Pyramid. It is for this concern they also gave us *the rest of the report,* after the conclusion or overview statement. The other 999 pages (or whatever) are the support—the guarantee that the top of page 1 is accurate. Your reader may choose not to read all those other pages of information, but their presence is comforting. It makes a reassuring statement—especially if it's easy to browse through. It almost invites the reader: "Come and look." But no one but you need ever know that you switched the order—except readers who are as smart as we are.

DEVIL'S ADVOCATE: In a speedreading course once I was told: If you're having trouble understanding something, stop trying to read in detail; browse through first, then read. You'll understand better. And it works.

GURU: Sure it works. But listen to what the reading experts are saying: "Hey, reader, just in case the writer didn't give you an overview, go in and construct your own."

DEVIL'S ADVOCATE: But the *writer* should do it, not the reader.

GURU: Of course. That's what the Inverted Pyramid structure is all about.

DEVIL'S ADVOCATE: Isn't there an H with the five W's of journalism?

GURU: That's the *How;* it's the rest of the article (or report). And there you have the classic organizing formula for a newspaper article: Five W's and an H. *Who, What, When, Where,* and *Why* in the opening paragraph, and the rest of the article tells *How.* That's the same as our advice: Start with the conclusion, then spend the rest of the report supporting it. In the real world, you may not always have all of the W's. But it seems to me the opening statement will always contain at least two: *What* and *Why.*

Incidentally, we said the W's go in the opening *paragraph,* not sentence. Think generally of two or three sentences for Who, What, When, Where, and Why.

DEVIL'S ADVOCATE: You said the three ways of arranging the rest of the information, after the overview statement, are order of importance, logical order, or chronological order. What is meant by *logical* order? Are we talking about formal logic?

GURU: It could be. For example, in a research report a scientist might use, say, syllogistic deduction, or some other specific logic plan, to prove something is true. Or you might use process of elimination to prove a decision is best—by proving all other choices are flawed. Or, the logic could be less formal—grouping the information in some planned order that serves some planned purpose.

DEVIL'S ADVOCATE: The *Summary* may contain a full page of information, but the *Conclusion* only 50 to 100 words? Why? What's the story?

GURU: The story is simple. This limit is sort of a proficiency test for writers, to protect readers. Remember, the reader is coming from the top down, but the *writer* is working from the bottom up. Okay? So, by the time the writer has progressed this far toward the front, he or she has already done all of the work being reported in the body, and most of the writing of the *whole* report. If, after all that, he or she can't tell what's really important in a few clear sentences, surely something must be wrong with the thinking. That writer isn't ready yet to write the most important sections of all—the up-front (overview) sections. That writer needs to start thinking: "What's the one statement about which I would be willing to say: '*It's all right if my reader reads nothing else.*' "

DEVIL'S ADVOCATE: The eight sections of a formal report create some needless repetition.

GURU: Repetition yes, needless no. It doesn't add much to the overall length of a major report, and it sets up a neat Inverted Pyramid for the reader—for the noblest of purposes: quicker reading and better understanding.

DEVIL'S ADVOCATE: You referred to *Appendixes.* Not *Appendices?*

GURU: Please, English is not Latin, okay? You people wear me out. I had a student once, a brilliant scientist and a nice guy, but a little nutty, who worked backward from the word *appendices* and concluded its singular is *appendicee.* But I don't know how he spelled it. You people really wear me out.

CHAPTER 7

REVIEW

How alert were you? All of these important points were discussed in the chapter you just read. You should be able to answer them all. If you cannot, it's in your interest to look them up.

What one statement sums up the advice on organizing expository writing?

The Inverted Pyramid structure gives the reader three choices, all good. Please describe them.

What are the three ways of arranging the body of a report, after the opening?

Which of those is usually the most desirable for the reader?

What is the best advice for ending a report?

Why is a reader better able to read the entire report after having had the overview first?

For what two reasons do writers often resist writing Inverted Pyramids?

Please list the eight sections of a formal report, in the order in which the reader reads them.

What is the difference between that order and the order in which the writer must write them?

PRACTICE

Readers want the conclusion first.

CHAPTER 7
EXERCISES

Exercise 23.

The Inverted Pyramid structure helps readers by giving the most important information as quickly as possible, in as little reading as possible. The hardest thing about writing in the Inverted Pyramid (expository) form is planning: What should be the opening—the one statement, or short group of statements, that sums up the whole piece of writing?

The memo below is well written in its words and sentences, but it is poorly organized; the writer simply put things down in the order they happened. That's a common mistake, because it's easy—almost like a fairy tale beginning *"Once upon a time . . ."* and ending *"They all lived happily ever after."*

Restructure the memo so it gives the reader the most important information first:

> *Bumstead Tool Company opened a credit card account with us on July 15, 1994. In October 1994 they began falling behind in payments.*
>
> *After sending them the MA and SD groups of collection letters, we put the company on our delinquent list and canceled their credit. At that time they owed $2,372.09. I phoned Mr. H. D. Bumstead, company president, on April 2, and he promised to send us the full amount within 30 days. I also requested that the company return our three credit cards.*
>
> *That was 30 days ago. We have received the credit cards but no money.*
>
> *This customer shows no willingness to cooperate. The Retail Credit Bureau reports they are unable to pay other bills. I recommend that this account be turned over to our legal department for further action.*
>
> *Mr. Bumstead was formerly sales manager of Western Tool Company, a good customer of ours for many years. He formed Bumstead Tool Company July 1, 1994.*

Your Rewrite

____

____

____

____

____

(Continued on next page)

EXERCISE 23 Your rewrite (continued):

Recommended

PRACTICE

Putting the conclusion first is easy.

Exercise 24.

The memo below is structured as a narrative, starting with introductory information and leading in logical order to its most important statement *at the end.* One simple change corrects this. Make that change, rearranging the information into the Inverted Pyramid structure:

> *Most designers believe that stress figures obtained from photographs are more accurate than those computed electronically. This is probably because photointerpretation is more complicated and takes longer. However, in many cases electronic results are more accurate.*
>
> *Analysts have the training necessary to determine which method will give the most accurate results for a particular job. They, not the designers, should decide whether photointerpretation or electronic data should be used. Please instruct all designers in your branch that they should not specify the method of measuring stress data in future reports on aircraft testing.*

Your Rewrite

Recommended

Exercise 25.

THIS IS THE BACKGROUND: Many companies in recent years have set up a department whose purpose is to analyze and evaluate other departments. This is usually called the Systems and Procedures Department, Operations Research, Management Services Audit, etc. Its staff members are usually experts at spotting troubles and recommending solutions.

In the LTT Scanner Division, this Department is called the Systems and Procedures Branch (S&P). The manager reports directly to the vice president of operations. LTT is a leading manufacturer of heavy duty medical scanners and is known for high quality products and reliable service. The home office is in Ithaca, N.Y., with manufacturing plants there and in St. Louis. Sales and service offices exist in major cities throughout the United States, Canada, and Mexico.

As S&P increased in size and scope at LTT the past few years, other departments began to regard its activities with suspicion. Today, depending on whom you talk to, S&P is called everything from "A necessary evil" to "a bunch of half-ass college-bred snoopers." Almost every management-level employee has heard by word of mouth that the department raises havoc with work routines when it undertakes investigations; that its recommended methods are usually less efficient than the old way; and that even if the new way is more efficient, it does not save enough to justify the cost of operating the S&P department. "Our savings are paying their salaries" has been a frequent complaint.

When S&P employees go out into the field to study an operation, the instructions from Ithaca are that they should be given full cooperation. But regional managers often take the attitude that no news from the home office is good news—especially when S&P is concerned. Such managers do little to conceal that attitude from the employees beneath them. As a result, the S&P auditors encounter resistance more often than cooperation.

Recently, Gayle Timmons and Harold Giardino, two young auditors from the Systems and Procedures Department, were assigned to do a systems and cost analysis of the work involved in receiving and answering a typical service call in the Salt Lake City Regional Office. Why Salt Lake City? Because records at the home office showed that service costs were lower there than in any other Region. Salt Lake City must be doing something LTT's other Regions could profit from learning.

The usual announcement went out to the regional manager announcing that the S&P auditors would be arriving, and it made clear that the company expected them to be given full cooperation in anything they requested.

Monday morning Timmons and Giardino arrived, expecting to spend a full week. They wanted to talk to the manager, several sales representatives, the repair crews, and the order clerks.

They spent the first morning with the regional manager, touring the operation and being introduced to other key personnel. Everything was cordial. But at lunch, which was the first time they were alone with the manager, they sensed hostility. After 45 minutes of small talk, he admitted the entire staff was not too happy when they received the announcement that S&P was going to examine every operation; their presence, it was widely believed, implied that the people in Ithaca doubted everyone's skills—from management down. The auditors tried to explain that the opposite was true, that the home office wanted to point up Salt Lake City as a **good example** for the other regions to follow—and in that sense their presence should be considered a compliment. Still, the manager was skeptical, and it showed. He assured them, however, that he had instructed everyone in the Region to cooperate in anything required of them for the survey.

"Oh, by the way," the manager said as they were getting up from lunch, "don't be upset by the hospital service manager. He's been here 16 years, and his repair crews are the best in the West. But he's touchy about criticism." The manager seemed edgy. The S&P auditors, comparing notes later, both sensed he was afraid they were going to louse things up.

Tuesday morning Timmons and Giardino were finally able to talk with the service manager. He talked politely about fishing in Utah and a few other trivial subjects. But when they tried to talk business, he seemed unwilling to listen to their explanation of the purpose of their study, let alone cooperate with them. He could not prevent them from talking to the repair and calibration crews, but he made it clear he did not expect they would learn much. "We'll cooperate," he reassured them. "My people are good enough they can give you anything you want without slowing down a bit."

The repair and calibration personnel were obviously talented, well trained, and well managed. They too, however, did not believe the true purpose of the S&P visit. They seemed friendly, even joking with the visitors. Or were they joking *at* them? It soon became obvious they weren't going to tell much—at least not in language the home office dudes from the East could understand. One of them even commented on the third day, when the visitors accompanied them on hospital calls, they didn't have much respect for (1) young college kids and (2) people who come around as experts in digital scanner repair but can't repair or calibrate one.

Although Timmons and Giardino were intimately familiar with all aspects of the design, manufacture, and marketing of heavy duty digital scanners, it was true they could not perform routine service on one. So they spent three hours Wednesday night studying a service manual—even memorizing the names of the parts. In this way they hoped to win the cooperation of the best repairmen in the West. To win acceptance from the department manager, they also decided to appeal to his interest in fishing; they bought outdoors magazines at the hotel newsstand and spent several more hours reading them.

Thursday and Friday the auditors were slightly more successful. But as they headed home Friday night and began planning their report, both agreed their S&P study had been seriously hampered by the attitude of the entire Salt Lake City group. As a result, the information they were bringing back was rather shallow, and they could probably not make recommendations that would benefit the other Regions. The week's trip was probably not worth the effort.

END OF BACKGROUND.

YOUR ASSIGNMENT: You are one of those S&P auditors. The two of you have decided you should be the one to write the report to management on this trip.

The heart of the lesson is this: To provide a proper overview, the opening paragraph should be a highly condensed summary of *all* the main points contained in the whole report—the information about which you would be willing to say, "It's all right if my reader reads nothing else." (This is the essence of the Inverted Pyramid theory; remember, the writer's job is to convey as much information as possible, as clearly and accurately as possible, *in as little reading as possible.*)

Your full Salt Lake City report, therefore, would certainly contain, among other things, sections stating in detail that the project failed, why it failed, and what should be done about it. Those are surely the most important things your reader needs to know. They are, then, the things that should appear (briefly) in your overview statement, or summary. The rest of the report gives the supporting details, and it should include all other pertinent information about the project.

DO NOT WRITE a full formal report with the eight sections discussed on page 104; that would be too much for this situation. Your trip report can be in the form of a memo, or a short report with just a few sections. **Suggestion:** Write the full opening paragraph (overview). Then just write the section headings for the topics you think should be discussed.

Remember: The purpose of this exercise is to evaluate the clarity and structure of your writing, not your ability to analyze the business problem and arrive at the best solution—**how** you write, not **what** you write.

Your Rewrite

"The outline, or plotline, is the architecture of writing; the words and sentences are the interior decoration."

—Ernest Hemingway

CHAPTER 8

SENSE AND NONSENSE ABOUT PLANNING (PRE-WRITING)

> The solution to any problem relies first on understanding what causes it, and this is certainly true of the writing problem many people complain is the hardest of all: getting started and writing productively. They fumble, they fuss, and the uneasy feeling in their minds just won't go away.

If you understand the reader's needs and the advantages of the Inverted Pyramid structure, organizing properly should not be difficult—at least, not for most short reports and letters. But structuring the ideas thoughtfully becomes much more of a challenge for larger writing jobs, such as major reports. And, of course, they are the ones that most need careful structuring.

Ironically, the most conscientious writers usually have the greatest trouble getting started. Careless people usually have no trouble at all with this part of the job, but thoughtful writers do—because they want to start correctly. They recognize, consciously or subconsciously, something immensely important in writing: *The way you treat the beginning of a letter or report will determine the character of the whole piece.* Or, as the old saying goes, "As the twig is bent, so grows the tree." That is certainly true in expository writing. So, wisely, the careful writer tries to begin his or her expository trip in the right direction.

Pointing in that right direction is one of the pivotal challenges of writing. Typically, the novice writer who doesn't yet walk with the *literati* sits down the first day of a major writing job with marvelous intentions. Then what? Nothing happens, if that writer is typical and trying hard to find the right opening; he or she sits staring at a blank page, mind wandering, grasping, in search of mental roadmaps for the writing trip. After 15 or 20 minutes the wanderer gives up. "I'll write it tomorrow" is everybody's surrender slogan. When you are that wanderer, tomorrow comes and you are no better able to write. You put it off a second day, then a third and fourth.

Eventually, you do write that report. When? At the deadline.

You are not alone if you have been able to do your best writing only under the pressure of the deadline. Even outstanding professional writers have often reported this about themselves.

What is it about deadlines that helps us get started? What does the deadline force you to do differently?

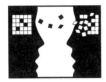

How to Outsmart the Deadline

This simple experiment demonstrates why most people have trouble getting started writing, and why they actually *can* write more productively when the deadline arrives. It will demonstrate something interesting and useful about how the brain—your brain—processes information.

Ask a friend how many different combinations (permutations) can be made of the letters A and B, and to name them (always using both letters and never repeating a letter). There are two: AB and BA.

Now ask that person how many combinations can be made A, B, and C, and to name them—*WITHOUT WRITING THEM.* There are six: ABC, ACB, BAC, BCA, CAB, and CBA. (An easy way to remember: Note there are three possible starting letters, and for each one we flip-flop the second and third. Mathematicians call this pattern *three factorial.*)

In classrooms, only about one out of five people can recite the six combinations of A, B, and C.

Next, ask how many combinations are possible with A, B, C, and D (four factorial), and ask your victim to recite them—*again without writing.* There are 24: ABCD, ABDC, ACBD, ACDB, ADBC, ADCB, BACD, BADC, BCAD, BCDA, BDAC, BDCA, CABD, CADB, CBAD, CBDA, CDAB, CDBA, DABC, DACB, DBAC, DBCA, DCAB, and DCBA. (Note that the pattern is basically the same as three factorial, above; but for each starting letter there are six sets of four, and in each set there is one more step.) Reciting the 24 combinations of A, B, C, and D is almost impossible, no matter how long one tries. *But with a pencil and paper most people can list them in less than four minutes.*

This experiment illustrates an important point about the human brain. As an isolated organ it has a surprising limitation: All of us can examine both combinations of A and B. But only about one of five intelligent adults can examine all six combinations of A, B, and C. And practically nobody can picture, and recite, the 24 possible combinations of A, B, C, and D. **Using his or her brain alone, as an isolated organ, then, the average intelligent adult is capable of examining all possible combinations of surprisingly few ideas—often as few as two, rarely more than three—even when those ideas are as simple as A, B, and C.**

But when you use a pencil and paper—when the brain can *see* the ideas as it tries to arrange them, there is a dramatic increase in the number of concepts it can examine intelligently.

What is the lesson here?

When we try to recite the 24 possible combinations of A, B, C, and D without looking at them, we are forcing the brain to operate as an isolated organ. But why try? It is not an isolated organ. It came with five senses attached. Only when the computer-brain receives input through its sensory channels—and especially the eyes—does it function as the world's most magnificent computer. The five senses are sight, hearing, touch, smell, and taste—probably in that order of importance in human evolution. By far the most useful for processing information is sight. The brain and the eyes together get the planning job done. Next best is the brain and the ears.

This explanation is needed. The eye has no advantage over the ear as an input to the brain, but the written word has a major advantage over the spoken word: It stays there, allowing the receiver to receive, examine, and re-examine the ideas at his or her own comfortable pace. The spoken word exists only the split second it is spoken, and so the receiver must examine the ideas at the sender's pace, and only once. For this reason, we will always be able to do our best thinking when we can see the ideas—literally *see* them, through our eyes, on a piece of paper. (But if you must plan ideas and can't write them down—driving somewhere, for example—talk to yourself. Aloud. Speak the ideas, including your doubts and concerns. And as you listen you'll be surprised how much more clearly you can arrange the ideas. And so, when you observe others talking to themselves you'll never again think they're strange.)

The Importance of the False Start

What does all this have to do with getting started in the writing process? **We have seen that most people have difficulty getting started because they are trying, conscientiously, to start correctly.** To figure out the best way to start, however, the struggling, wandering writer must examine more than just the beginning; he or she must examine beginning, middle, and end—and all possible combinations of all the ideas—to decide what is the *best* combination. When you are sitting there, staring at a blank piece of paper until the deadline comes, you're trying to do that mentally, without being able to *see* the ideas as the brain needs to see them.

We have shown with the A-B-C experiment, however, that you probably are not capable of doing that, even when those ideas are the simplest known and have the clearest possible logical relationships. The memory is not good enough; the struggler/wanderer gets lost. The brain needs to SEE the ideas to be able to arrange them intelligently. No wonder so many writers flounder trying to get started when they try to organize the ideas in the brain!

But where else to organize them?

What does the deadline change? Until the last desperate moment, the conscientious struggler/wanderer is hoping to start correctly. But this means planning the order of the ideas first, and we have already shown that we cannot do that in the brain alone. It is physiologically impossible; the brain needs something to *look* at. Unable to be productive, you keep putting the writing off. Finally, the deadline demands that you start writing something; *at this point any start becomes better than none, even if it's wrong.* And now for the first time, you begin doing what needs to be done, the way it needs to be done. For the first time, you force yourself to put something—anything—down on paper—perhaps grudgingly. AND THEN: As you produce, then read what you have produced, your eyes begin providing information to the brain the way the brain must receive it in order to establish complex relationships. Even if the various ideas are in the wrong order, you can then picture clearly what should have been the correct order. And lo, the struggler/wanderer begins resembling a writer.

One of the most important lessons in all of writing, then, is: **The false start (wandering, trying to find the way) is the necessary first step in serious writing.**

When the deadline comes, you get desperate enough to say: "I've got to get started or I'm in trouble. If it's wrong, I'll correct it later." So you start writing, conceding that what comes out will probably be pretty confused and need to be rearranged. *As the writing progresses, you are creating that false start—something for your brain to look at and correct.* Then, at some point you begin picturing what the proper order should be—how you should have organized the writing in the first place. You can do this because your brain takes over as a computer. You then simply reorganize what you have written.

But wait. Writing a report the wrong way to find out what should have been the right way? This wastes time and work. There is the delay of staring at the blank page, and all of the wasted work—yours and the typist's—in writing, then organizing, then rewriting. **Still, that FALSE START—getting something down on paper so you can look at it and rearrange it—IS the necessary first step.** But there must be a way to make that false start at the beginning, without all the delay, and without all of the wasted time and work. Of course, there is such a way: *Make false starts in skeleton structure.* What are we leading up to? What is the skeleton structure of writing? THE OUTLINE.

Here then, finally, is the hated word. Outline, outline, outline! It is the most important single step in writing—whether you are writing a letter, an engineering report, or the greatest novel ever written.

Yes, novelists outline too. The popular impression is that the novelist sits down at the word processor and fills page one, then plans what will happen on page two, and so on, filling wastebaskets as he or she progresses. No, no. That wasn't true even when novelists (as recent as W. Somerset Maugham) wrote manuscripts by hand. Filling wastebaskets, yes. But not knowing where the story is going? Unthinkable. The novelist first develops the plot carefully in outline form. This is called the *plotline,* or *storyline.* Only when he or she feels comfortable with that story in skeleton form—from beginning to end in considerable detail—does the professional writer begin expanding it into words and sentences. Only then can he or she decide whether it's *worth* expanding into words and sentences.

Ernest Hemingway addressed this in his advice to young writers. He told them that the plotline or outline determines the value of WHAT you write. It is here, then, that you determine whether or not you will win literary awards. The outline (plotline), Hemingway said, is the architecture of writing; words and sentences are just the interior decoration.

Notice Hemingway is acknowledging that great writing depends first on valuable, well-planned ideas—and only then on the writer's skill at choosing words and building them into sentences. He guarded his time jealously, hoping to spend as much of it as possible observing the rich experiences of the world, and participating in them; these were the sources of his storylines. And that strategy allowed him to express them, in his unique style of artistry, with as little time as possible needed for the important job of rewriting. Again, the total separation between WHAT is written (the *art*) and HOW it is written (the *craft*).

(By the way, have you noticed, while reading this chapter, where its conclusion came? The conclusion, or overview, is: *You must outline before you write.* But you were led to this gradually. Why? Remember, Chapter 7 emphasized that the conclusion should normally go at the beginning, *unless it is so negative it*

Infamous Quotation No. 2

U.S. education has been under severe criticism since the 1970's for failing to teach basic skills. English teachers have been particularly singled out, as writing skills have declined. But not all English teachers agree they should teach writing.

At an education conference on literacy in Columbus, Ohio in 1993, a high school English Teacher said (and his colleagues agreed): "Helping students improve their writing skills would be helping corporate America to exploit them. If they're good writers they're more productive employees, and the hidden agenda is corporate profit. Literacy is 'global citizenship,' and that is our mission in today's cultural environment."

That remains overwhelmingly the prevailing attitude today.

(Also see: Infamous Quotation No. 1, page 15.)

would close the reader's mind to reason. Outlining is certainly that unpopular a subject; most people object to reading or hearing anything about it. For this reason, in the last several pages you were taken deliberately, gradually to that conclusion, to avoid the risk you might lose interest and stop reading. This is the only time in this book you have received [or will receive] direct advice in the *narrative,* not expository, form.)

Outline before you write. The brain—magnificent computer though it is—simply is not able to process complex ideas very well without the proper sensory input: the eyes. *The false start IS the necessary first step!*

The Real Way to Outline

Very well, then. You will outline. But most untrained writers, when they finally admit they really *need* to outline (usually after staring at a blank note pad for days), approach this by going through the serious ritual of placing in the upper left-hand corner:

I.

Then what? They sit and stare at *that* for days. The Roman Numeral did not provide Divine intervention; it's rare these days. The mental block did not go away.

No Roman Numerals, please. At least, not yet.

Remember, the first purpose of the outline is to allow yourself the luxury of the *False Start*—quickly, and with little wasted effort. Now consider: **The moment you put Roman Numeral I at the top of the page, you *deprived* yourself of that false start.** Truly, you are now in a worse state than when the page was bare; you have now committed yourself to writing first things first, second things second, etc. Before you could *write* them in that order, however, you would have to *think* them that way. But we have already shown with the ABC experiment that you cannot *think* the proper order of the ideas unless you can *see* them.

The only sensible FIRST outline is that FALSE START. Admit to yourself, and be comfortable admitting, that the first version of whatever you put down is going to serve the noble purpose of being *wrong*—something to look at and correct. It has to be that way for most of us. Music scholars claim that Wolfgang Amadeus Mozart could write complete symphonies so skillfully in his mind that the first version he put on paper—all of the notes for all of the different instruments—often ended up the final version, and some extremely gifted writers may be able to create novels (or business reports) that skillfully. Most of us can't. So the thoughtful writer puts as little time or effort into the first version as possible. Simply list the ideas on the page in random order. Imagine you tilt your head forward and let every idea you can think of on this subject spill out onto the page. Very little concern should be given at this point for proper order; don't even think yet about separating major from minor ideas. Just throw down a random list, almost like a pile of building materials, aware as you add ideas to the pile that, from them, eventually you are going to plan the structure you want. *And that structure will be: an Inverted Pyramid.* Here, now, your major effort begins, but the FALSE START procedure takes the wasted work—and time—out of it.

A pile of building materials—the materials you will assemble into a useful structure of information—which in turn will empower readers to receive that information, *your information,* accurately, intelligently, and easily. And in so doing, that structure will shine a spotlight on your thinking and writing skills, for readers to know and appreciate. BUT: Where do the various parts go?

The only things you know about positioning, at this point, are that a title will go at the beginning, that from the information you just deposited into a random list you will form the body, and you will open that body with a full and accurate overview statement. But what about the rest?

No builder begins construction without blueprints; to create something of value without them would almost certainly require much tearing apart and rebuilding. The FALSE START method of outlining allows writers to do that tearing apart and rebuilding without the wasted time and effort of writing things, then examining to find out what's wrong, then writing again repeatedly. Inexperienced writers revise in that cumbersome way, and when they do they are usually changing the *order* of the ideas, to improve the logical flow from idea to idea. The ABC experiment should have convinced you by now that such changes are a necessary part of the writing process; the first version of any expository piece will almost certainly *not* be in the order that best satisfies you, the writer. Nor will the second necessarily be the one. They are FALSE STARTS. And you will save much time, work, and anguish by making them in skeleton structure.

Once you have that random list (the false start) before you—and it can be very rough—your brain has something it can look at. Then your reward starts to come. From that point on you will find you can begin organizing intelligently, because the brain will now function as a computer. Now your mind will begin to see relationships as they should be. The first thing you may notice is that some of the ideas stand out as the major items, the ones that would have Roman numerals if you were using them. (And, very likely, some ideas are quickly discarded.) Now, accurate conclusions may start becoming more obvious. *Next step:* The thoughtful writer is looking by now for signposts—to help point the direction this information should be going. Now you may choose to try your first attempt at writing the overview statement. (But you will almost certainly change it later, possibly several times, as your thoughts become clearer.) Even though that first overview will probably not end up the final one, it will give you a direction—a path to follow as you try to arrange all your ideas from a random list to the outline you want. If that one doesn't satisfy, try other paths; very little work is wasted. A BATTLE has been won, because now you are thinking productively.

Next step: Separate the major items on your random list from the minor ones, then plan the order of those major items—the logical flow of your information from the overview statement to the bottom of the Inverted Pyramid. TOTAL VICTORY is near. Examine one arrangement, then another, until you become satisfied you have finally arrived at the one that best takes you where you want to go. Remember, you can change your mind at any time—filling wastebaskets as you go, but wastebaskets containing little wasted work. Gradually, you have refined false starts into nearly finished blueprints.

Now finish the outline. Go back to that original (random) list, and simply transfer each of the remaining (minor) ideas under the category it best fits. These relationships should be easy to see now. And if you have left out any information, major or minor, the gaps should be noticeable and easy to fill.

At this point, incidentally, you can add the Roman Numerals if you wish; they may help readers by quickly telling which are the main ideas and which are subordinate. But they can cause you, the writer, considerable harm in the early planning unless you put them in *after you have outlined.*

Sensible steps, then, for sensible outlining, are:

- Make a random list containing all the things you can think of, major and minor, that should be (or might be) part of this report or letter.
- Separate that list into major and minor items, and make a new list containing just the major ones. Then try to arrange this new list from beginning to end into the structure that best helps your reader. (See: Inverted Pyramid, page 97.) Change the order as often as you feel you can improve the flow; changes are exquisitely simple at this point.
- Finish this *first version* of the outline by inserting the minor items from the random list to the new list, under major categories where they belong. Add, delete, or change the order of any ideas as you see fit.
- Examine the whole outline again, looking for ways to improve the flow of information. Remember, the whole idea of the FALSE START is to make changes in skeleton structure, while they are easy, rather than in the finished writing.
- Keep adding, deleting, or changing as you see fit; revisions are so much faster and easier now than later.

And now you are ready to start the language skills part of writing.

Mind mapping. Some recent theorists advocate a method of organizing thoughts by putting them on paper in picture format, with key words radiating in all directions from the central idea (subject), rather than arranged in lists. A poster-sized sheet of paper is recommended, and bright colored pens, and the use of small pictures or symbols representing the individual (radiating) ideas. This process is described as *mind mapping* or *radiant thinking.* Its followers claim the process helps us realize our brain's full potential to think with both its left (analytical) and right (imaginative) hemispheres.

Perhaps mind mapping, for writers, at least, can be compared to the *first step* of outlining—the false start—but not the entire pre-writing process.

Comparing a writer's outline to a map seems worthwhile. Before putting the bags in the car and driving off on a long trip, most of us plan carefully and even draw the route, and mark our various stops, on a road map. But before marking that map, we must at least make a list of the places we want to visit. The FALSE START is still the necessary first step.

Many popular phrases have been used to describe the important process of structuring ideas into a working outline. In the late 1940's, World War II veterans returning from the armed forces brought with them the term *brainstorming,* a method used by military leaders to make important decisions by consensus. Those present would be asked to compile a list, on a chalk board or flip chart, of

Acronyms: Mercy to Your Reader

An acronym is a word made of the initials of a complex name or special term. Used properly, acronyms are symbols of kindness to your reader; they replace difficult terms with simple ones.

But they are simple only if known. Therefore, always spell out the full term the first time it appears in any piece of writing; then follow the fully spelled version immediately by the acronym (initials) in parentheses, almost as if saying, ". . . hereinafter referred to as. . . ." Example: *Pump output is measured in gallons per minute (GPM).*

Warning: Don't overuse acronyms. If a sentence or a page looks like a bowl of alphabet soup (*The CPHM reading in the WRG indicates a PNA and should be acted upon by the SOD. . . .*), you are being inconsiderate, not merciful, to your reader.

all factors that might be involved in a decision, then rank them by order of importance, discuss them, and arrive at a recommended strategy. They learned it was important to list those ideas on the chalk board or flip chart. Their brains needed to *see* the ideas in order to examine them intelligently and arrive at a consensus that represented the best thoughts of the experts present. The FALSE START was the necessary first step.

In the 1970's, the term *clustering* began appearing—listing all the ideas in related clusters. But how does the writer do that? How does his or her brain recognize those relationships without first being able to *see* them? Without understanding this, the would-be clusterer will sit staring at a blank page for days—until the deadline. The FALSE START remains the first step in planning the order of the ideas. How each writer progresses beyond that, from random thoughts to a finished outline, is to a large extent a matter of his or her own work habits.

Two hints to help you outline:

1. **Use a piece of scrap paper.** Remember, the first version must be a FALSE START. Perhaps it should be on a sheet of paper having heel marks or coffee rings, to remind you: *If it does not end in the wastebasket in a few minutes, you are not using it to your best advantage.* It should be something just to look at and correct—quickly and easily, in skeleton structure, then throw away.
2. **Use key word phrases.** While outlining, do *not* write the ideas in full sentences. You should not yet be thinking about picking the right words or building them into the best grammatical structures; that comes later. Focus now on WHAT to say, not HOW to say it.

Don't be misled, however. Experienced writers know that outlining is not easy or pleasant. The first step, the false start, should be easy—just putting down your random list of key word phrases. But then, structuring those into one carefully planned and intelligently related group of ideas may be the hardest part of the job. After all, it is here that you will do your major *thinking*. It is here that you will establish the logical flow of your ideas. It is here, then, that you will establish the *value* and ultimate success of WHAT you write.

Therefore, whether we like it or not, outlining is surely the most important step in any writing.

Outlining improves your word/sentence skill. This surprises many. By outlining, you will also be better able to select the right words and build them into sentences later, when you are finally ready for them. Why? Because, by outlining we are dividing writing into its two major elements—*what* we write and *how* we write it—and allowing ourselves to concentrate on each separately. Both are so demanding that it seems unthinkable anyone could address them at the same time and give both the attention they need. Addressed separately, your ideas will be more intelligently thought out, and your words and sentences will probably be clearer and more eloquent.

How long should it take? Give up the pipe dream that outlining is a five-minute job. Sometimes it may indeed take just minutes, or it may take three-quarters of your total writing time. (Remind yourself, however: If you're having

The Hippopotamus Joke

This zoo manager was about to be fired. The trouble was, the zoo needed two hippopotamuses, but the ZM kept putting off ordering them because even most ZM's don't know whether to say *hippopotamuses* or *hippopotami*.

When you get desperate enough, though, you often find a way. On the last desperate day, the triumphant ZM wrote the hippopotamus company (or wherever you buy hippopotamuses):

"Gentlemen, Will you please send to the undersigned one healthy adult hippopotamus," then signed the letter. Then: "P.S.—as long as you're sending one, make it two."

Moral: There is a right way of saying anything, but you usually don't find it by piling more junk on the wrong way.

(Also see: The Penguin Joke, page 7.)

(Also see Salutations, Gentlemen, page 141.)

trouble with the order of the ideas, imagine how much worse it would be to try selecting the right words and build sentences at the same time.) *In general, a 1:1 ratio may be reasonable; plan on spending as much time outlining as writing.* For most people, that would mean dividing their time differently—more time planning, less time writing. **But you will usually save in *total* time through this rearrangement.** More important, the finished product is likely to be better organized and better written.

How detailed should it be? Only you can decide. Certainly, any useful outline must contain all of your *major* ideas in their proper order—those that would have the *Roman Numerals* in a traditional outline. How far you plan the outline beyond that is mostly a matter of your own work habits. Of one thing you can be sure: The more detailed the outline, the better organized and more clearly written the finished product will be, and the quicker and easier your writing job will be.

DEVIL'S ADVOCATE: Heel marks or coffee rings?

GURU: I recommend both, actually. They serve as an announcement reminding you: *If this sheet doesn't end up in the wastebasket very soon, you aren't using it correctly.* Remember, the first thing you put on paper is going to be a FALSE START; you don't get the choice. We simply can't plan the best order of the ideas in our minds, so we need to put them down in a *wrong* order so we can SEE what should have been the *right* order, then correct it. The choice we get is whether to correct it quickly in skeleton structure, drawing arrows back and forth, or by writing a whole report to find out what was wrong, then correct that. Repeat after me: "FALSE START," six times.

DEVIL'S ADVOCATE: With computers, changing the order of large blocks of text is easy. So I just start with a rough draft and make changes as I see the need. Computers are hot; outlines are not. So what's the big deal?

GURU: Listen, if you want to be the guru, go ahead, but right now I am, so *no rough drafts.* Here's why: When you sit down to write with the attitude, "There's no sense trying very hard because the first version isn't going to be very good anyhow . . . ," it probably won't be. The order of the ideas will probably be wrong, or you may do less than your best in choosing words and building sentences. Or both. So you end up with a lot of—may I say *junk?* Also remember, in order to rearrange the sections properly, and quickly, you need to see them all at once. Otherwise you can't sense how one change will affect other sections. The idea of the FALSE START is to *reduce work,* not create more, but the rough draft deprives you of that advantage. Trust me; I'm your friend.

CHAPTER 8

REVIEW

How alert were you? All of these important points were discussed in the chapter you just read. You should be able to answer them all. If you cannot, it's in your interest to look them up.

Why do most intelligent adults have trouble getting started on major writing jobs?

____

____

The brain has a surprising limitation that affects your ability to organize ideas. Please describe it.

____

____

Most people do their best writing only at the deadline. Why? What does the deadline force you to do differently?

____

____

The ____________ ____________ is the necessary first step in writing.

As a guide, what proportion of your total writing time should you reasonably expect to spend outlining?

____

What is the objection to using Roman Numerals as you begin outlining?

____

____

How will outlining improve your ability to pick the right words and build them into clear, precise sentences?

____

____

Outlining will almost always save you time. True or false? ____________

PRACTICE
The FALSE START Outline.

CHAPTER 8
EXERCISES

Exercise 26.

Outlining is the most important single step in writing.

Imagine you are going to write a report on the subject of *flextime,* a system many companies and government agencies are adopting, which allows employees to choose their own working hours. You have just listed all the ideas you can think of on the subject, in random order as they came into your head. That list appears below; it is your false start:

Less absenteeism and tardiness
Scheduling is difficult
Steps to be taken in advance
Rules printed and distributed
Increases personal freedom for employees with special needs
Objectives must be defined
Management support needed
Slows down communications
Smith Kline Corporation
Improves public image
Hourly employees may complain
Many large users
Raises employee morale
Reduces cafeteria congestion
Hewlett-Packard
Coordinator must be appointed
Makes personnel recruitment easier
Department of Transportation
Reduced parking lot congestion
Metropolitan Life Insurance
Employee briefing needed
Reduces turnover
U.S. Department of Agriculture
Hours must be limited
Expands hours customers can phone us.

(Continued on next page)

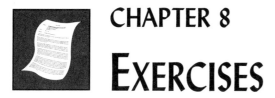

PRACTICE

EXERCISE 26 (continued):

As you examine the random list of ideas related to flextime, you begin to **see** relationships you could not envision before. The ideas clearly fall into four categories. Those categories are:

Your Version

Recommended

EXERCISE 26 (continued):

Now outline the rest of the report. List those four main categories by order of importance, then under each one place its minor ideas from the main list. Now, for the first time, you are ready to write the report, expanding the ideas fully into words and sentences. (But you need not write the whole report for this exercise.) After you have outlined, the hardest work is done.

I. ______________________________

II. ______________________________

III. ______________________________

IV. ______________________________

(Continued on next page)

PRACTICE

EXERCISE 26 (continued):

The four main categories by order of importance, with the minor ideas listed under each one:

Recommended

I. ______________________________

____

____

____

____

____

____

II. ______________________________

____

____

____

____

____

____

III. ______________________________

____

____

____

____

____

____

IV. ______________________________

____

____

____

____

____

____

(Continued on next page)

EXERCISE 26 (continued):

PRACTICE

Now, as you examine those four major categories and the individual thoughts listed under them, you should begin to see things about them you couldn't see before. Does one of the major ideas stand out? Or does some new idea suggest itself? Perhaps now you can begin to see what your **overview** statement should be. (Remember, the Inverted Pyramid demands that you start with the one statement or group of statements that sums up the whole report.)

In the imaginary report on page 129, what should be your opening statement, or overview? It can be more than one sentence:

Your Version

Recommended

"The great enemy of clear language is insecurity."

—George Orwell

CHAPTER 9

FINISHING TOUCHES OF THE PROS

A few simple preparations can help your reader to absorb your information, by making the pages containing that information easy to read. These are perhaps the final part of your work. Writers often take great pains to organize well and write clearly, only to weaken the effect—sometimes severely—by failing to do these simple things correctly. The last five percent of the job, the supporting mechanical part, weakens the heart of your work.

Headings: Readers Love Them

Probably the most important of mechanical considerations is the use of headings. They're easy to use, and they immediately add a touch of professionalism. Consider using headings in all reports. The longer the report, the more helpful they are to the reader. (But don't use them in letters; headings make a letter look like a form letter, and readers resent that.)

Your headings help the reader three ways. First, they provide overviews along the way; they announce each key point *before* its detailed discussion. Remember, readers understand the details better knowing in advance what they are going to receive. Second, those little signposts along the way help the reader to read selectively—choosing to stop at some passages but not others. And third, headings give the reader places to stop temporarily, to regroup your thoughts or to rest.

The use of headings will also help you, the writer, by relieving you of the need to write transition passages, which are often hard to write. Those few words provide all the transition readers need. They allow you to flow smoothly and easily from the end of one major idea to the beginning of the next.

What should your headings be, and where should they go? If you outlined properly, you have already written them. Just take those key word phrases from your finished, carefully planned outline and deposit them into the report. You will be pleasantly surprised how easy this is and how effective they will be—road signs readers appreciate while hardly being aware of their presence.

Here you see a sample of a page that is set up thoughtfully for the reader. It uses headings, and there is white space at the paragraph breaks:

The Question Mark

People know how to use question marks properly; you end questions with them, as you end sentences with periods. The trouble is, most writers don't use questions in their writing. Why not? They are as useful in writing as in speech, and there is little reason to deprive yourself of them.

The Exclamation Point

Most writers should not need the exclamation point very often. But when you need it, how marvelously it performs! An exclamation point is a period with a bang. Not much of a bang, but enough that it signals to the reader that the writer wanted emphasis here.

Quotation Marks

Generally speaking, use quotation marks only for quotations—and this means you are repeating the *exact* words of the person being quoted. Always use them in pairs. Use single quotation marks for a quotation within a quotation. (On most word processing programs and typewriters the apostrophe is used for this.)

We say *generally speaking* because some writers use quotation marks another way—not for quotations but to notify the reader that a word or phrase is being used in some unusual way: *The air seemed "stuffy" after the storm.* The writer seems almost to be apologizing for using the word. This usage of quotation marks is questionable, but most language authorities tolerate it. A wise attitude might be: If you have to apologize very often for using words, you're probably not choosing them very well.

The Hyphen

Use hyphens to divide words that won't fit at the end of a line. Here, a bit of common sense is called for. Breaking a word this way is generally undesirable, and if you can avoid breaking one by lengthening (or shortening) a line by a few letters, you should do so (unless producing flush right margins on a computer). If you must divide a word, do so only between syllables (indicated in dictionaries by a dot between letters).

Use hyphens also to connect the words of a compound adjective if the absence of the hyphen could cause misunderstanding: *The model 4000 comes complete with four-channel indicators* (indicators with four channels). There is a great difference between that and: *The model 4000 comes complete with four channel indicators* (four indicators of channels). Compound adjectives may be more than two words: *Ready-to-wear clothing, faster-than-average production rate, seventy-six-year-old marathon runner.*

Notice how easy the information is to read with headings, and how attractive and professional they make the pages look.

To demonstrate the importance of headings, that same passage is shown on the following page without them—with just white space where the headings were before:

People know how to use question marks properly; you end questions with them, as you end sentences with periods. The trouble is, most writers don't use questions in their writing. Why not? They are as useful in writing as in speech, and there is little reason to deprive yourself of them.

Most writers should not need the exclamation point very often. But when you need it, how marvelously it performs! An exclamation point is a period with a bang. Not much of a bang, but enough that it signals to the reader that the writer wanted emphasis here.

Generally speaking, use quotation marks only for quotations—and this means you are repeating the *exact* words of the person being quoted. Always use them in pairs. Use single quotation marks for a quotation within a quotation. (On most word processing programs and typewriters the apostrophe is used for this.)

We say *generally speaking* because some writers use quotation marks another way—not for quotations but to notify the reader that a word or phrase is being used in some unusual way: *The air seemed "stuffy" after the storm.* The writer seems almost to be apologizing for using the word. This usage of quotation marks is questionable, but most language authorities tolerate it. A wise attitude might be: If you have to apologize very often for using words, you're probably not choosing them very well.

Use hyphens to divide words that won't fit at the end of a line. Here, a bit of common sense is called for. Breaking a word this way is generally undesirable, and if you can avoid breaking one by lengthening (or shortening) a line by a few letters, you should do so (unless producing flush right margins on a computer). If you must divide a word, do so only between syllables (indicated in dictionaries by a dot between letters).

Use hyphens also to connect the words of a compound adjective if the absence of the hyphen could cause misunderstanding: *The model 4000 comes complete with four-channel indicators* (indicators with four channels). There is a great difference between that and: *The model 4000 comes complete with four channel indicators* (four indicators of channels). Compound adjectives may be more than two words: *Ready-to-wear clothing, faster-than-average production rate, seventy-six-year-old marathon runner.*

Here is the same information again, with neither white space nor headings—just one solid glob lying there waiting for the reader:

People know how to use question marks properly; you end questions with them, as you end sentences with periods. The trouble is, most writers don't use questions in their writing. Why not? They are as useful in writing as in speech, and there is little reason to deprive yourself of them. Most writers should not need the exclamation point very often. But when you need it, how marvelously it performs! An exclamation point is a period with a bang. Not much of a bang, but enough that it signals to the reader that the writer wanted emphasis here. Generally speaking, use quotation marks only for quotations—and this means you are repeating the *exact* words of the person being quoted. Always use them in pairs. Use single quotation marks for a quotation within a quotation. (On most word processing programs and typewriters the apostrophe is used for this.) We say *generally speaking* because some writers use quotation marks another way—not for quotations but to notify the reader that a word or phrase is being used in some unusual way: *The air seemed "stuffy" after the storm.* The writer seems almost to be apologizing for using the word. This usage of quotation marks is controversial, but most language authorities tolerate it. A wise attitude might be: If you have to apologize very often for using words, you're probably not choosing them very well. Use hyphens to divide words that won't fit at the end of a line. Here, a bit of common sense is called for. Breaking a word this way is generally undesirable, and if you can avoid breaking one by lengthening (or shortening) a line by a few letters, you should do so (unless producing flush right margins on a computer). If you must divide a word, do so only between syllables (indicated in dictionaries by a dot between letters). Use hyphens also to connect the words of a compound adjective if the absence of the hyphen could cause misunderstanding: *The model 4000 comes complete with four-channel indicators* (indicators with four channels). There is a great difference between that and: *The model 4000 comes complete with four channel indicators* (four indicators of channels). Compound adjectives may be more than two words: *Ready-to-wear clothing, faster-than-average production rate, seventy-six-year-old marathon runner.* Three spaced dots (and you should instruct the typist to put spaces between them) in a quotation tell the reader you have deliberately left out some of the words: *Abraham Lincoln said, "My paramount objective . . . is to save the union, and is not either to save or destroy slavery."* A little-known (and not very important) fact about ellipses: An ellipses is three dots to indicate the omission of words *in the middle* of a sentence. Four dots indicate that the omission continues *to the end* of a sentence; the fourth dot stands for the period.

Never present information that way to your reader. It is thoughtless and inconsiderate. The reader gets discouraged just seeing that coming.

The Importance of White Space

The next thing you can do to help readers, and to send a silent message about your writing skills, is to use plenty of white space. It, too, brings joy to readers. It is easy to use, inexpensive, and effective. Conscientious typists sometimes squeeze too much on a page, robbing you of white space, robbing your work of the deluxe presentation it deserves. Do not let them. Tell the typist to leave at least one inch of white space around all four sides of every sheet that ever leaves the computer printer or typewriter. Any good secretarial manual says margins should be at least one inch wide; be sure they are. That is the default (standard) setting in most word processing programs. Insist also on at least an inch of white space at major headings, to make them stand out. Remember, those headings need to be immediately noticeable—even to the scanning reader.

Also, be sure the typist skips a line between paragraphs, and if a letter is double-spaced, it should be triple-spaced between paragraphs; readers need a visible gap at the paragraph breaks. This is especially important as indented paragraphs become further obsolete in letters (or other printed material).

The writer must control these things. The typist has a tendency to try to save paper, and this is admirable, but the thoughtful writer's first concern must be something far more important than the cost of paper: the cost and the effectiveness of the ideas it carries.

Paragraph Structuring

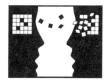

Paragraphs help the reader two ways. First, they present clusters of related sentences, and for this, they are important building blocks in your logic. A new paragraph suggests some break, or shift, in the logic, or a shift in time, or location, or some other kind of information. Second, and less commonly known, paragraphs provide eye muscle relief. The breaks allow readers to glance from the page for a split second and then find their place quickly and continue reading.

How long should paragraphs be? Generally, like sentences, keep them short; look for places to break them. Your paragraphs probably should average about seven or eight lines. But also like sentences, a good mixture is desirable. No minimum, and a maximum of 15 lines. Let the size and shape of the cluster of sentences determine the size and shape of the paragraph. Skip a line between paragraphs.

Reading experts point out that comprehension begins to drop after about 10 typewritten lines and drops drastically after about 15 lines. (Curiously, this is true regardless how wide the lines are.) If there is no logical breaking point after about 15 lines in a passage you are writing, break anyhow.

Each paragraph does *not* require a topic sentence. You may have learned it does, but that is too rigid a discipline.

Also, it is *not* true that a paragraph must contain more than one sentence. In fact, an effective way to emphasize an idea is to write it as a very short sentence and make it a separate paragraph. It practically jumps off the page. Don't do this very often, however.

(For other common misbeliefs, see page 52.)

Where Should Graphics Go?

Graphs, charts, tables, drawings, photographs, and other forms of non-verbal information are often an important part of expository writing, sometimes as important as the text itself—especially in reports. How you present them makes a difference to your reader, and that is mostly a matter of *where* you position them.

In a very short report (perhaps one to five pages), simply add them as attachments at the end, the same as you would for enclosures to a business letter.

But in a long report, never force your reader to go somewhere else to understand what he or she is reading, if you can avoid doing so. Usually you can. Put each graph, table, etc., in the body of the report—right on the page where you are discussing it, if possible. Put the graphics in an Appendix only when doing so creates an easier flow of information for the reader: (1) when there are so many graphics they would break up the report badly if interspersed throughout, or (2) when they are definitely unimportant (optional) reading.

Also, be sure to write a full, detailed caption for each graphic. Don't presume your readers can examine your information as intelligently as you can. In fact, you should probably presume the opposite. After all, *you* are the expert in your field; *you* probably gathered the information that went into those graphs, charts, or tables and are intimately familiar with the information they contain. The reader will benefit, in these captions, from your special help; each one should be an overview statement—a brief summary of the graphic. It may be as long as four or five lines. It should tell enough that the reader learns the highlights of the graph, chart, or table without studying it in detail and without reading about it in the text. This means you are doing some repeating, but only of key information. This kind of repetition is merciful, and it doesn't add much to the length. The graphic and its caption should be capable of standing alone, fully self-explanatory.

Ways To Add Emphasis (Italics, Boldface, Bullets)

Experienced writers know many ways to help readers by giving special emphasis to key words or short passages. When we talk, we intuitively raise or lower our voice, or gesture with our hands, or pause to emphasize key ideas to our listeners. You can—and should—do a few simple things to create similar effects with the written word. Some useful methods are: underlining, capital letters, boldface type, italics, or special type faces. Try these techniques if you are not accustomed to doing so.

In the past, typewriters gave us underlining or CAPITAL LETTERS; only commercial printers could use:

- **boldface type,**
- *italics,*
- special typefaces.

Today almost every word processor can give you boldface type, and if you have a modern printer, italics and special typefaces are also possible.

Use bullets (dots at the beginning of lines or paragraphs, as above) to emphasize several ideas presented consecutively as a series. Readers love them.

All of these tools of the thoughtful writer are used throughout this book—and in other books and magazines you have been reading all your life. It's surprising, however, how many ordinary people, when they write, overlook taking advantage of these useful tools that are so appreciated by readers.

Do not overuse these marvelous devices, however, or the effect is lost.

Fact and Fancy about Letters

All of the advice on clarity and structure presented in this book applies to letters as much as to any other kind of writing. Only a few things about letters are different from other kinds of writing, and those few things are simply procedural.

The Address Block. Include in this order: name; title; department (if you include one); company; street address; city, state, and zip code. Notice that the name of the person you are writing ordinarily belongs on the first line, not in an attention line at the bottom of the address block. Commonly, an attention line is used only when sending legal or financial documents to an organization.

The Subject Line. Do you need one? It may be useful, but include a subject line only if your company or department requires it, or you feel it serves some specific purpose. If it is required, it may benefit one of two people: the manager who scans outgoing letters written by subordinate employees, or the file clerk. But notice they are both at the *sending* end; your subject line is usually of no value to anyone at the receiving end; your letter will almost certainly be filed there under your name, or your company's, not by your subject line. Therefore, two rules are important for subject lines if you use them at all: (1) Keep them short. We said subject *line,* not paragraph. If this line gets longer than a few words, the file clerk gets different choices of subjects to file under, and the manager loses the chance to scan quickly and decide which letters to read. (2) Never refer to the subject line in the body of the letter. Doing so would penalize the reader by making him or her look two different places for the information. This means you may never refer to the *above subject customer,* or the *above subject equipment,* or the above subject anything.

The Salutation. Somehow, some people manage often to use the wrong one. Use the name of the person you are writing if you know it: *Dear Mr. Wilton.* And by the way, it is perfectly proper to address a person by first name in a dignified business letter—but only if you would normally do so face to face. Never use *Dear Sir,* or *Gentlemen.* If you are writing to a person by title but do not have that person's name (formerly the *Dear Sir* situation), use his or her title in the salutation: *Dear Sales Manager,* or *Dear Research Director.* If you have neither a name nor a title (formerly the *Gentlemen* situation), *Dear Reader* seems to be the best the experts have been able to recommend. *Dear Sir or Madam,* or *Gentlepersons,* just will not do. One suggestion: A simple phone call to a telephone operator or secretary will usually give you the information you need for a more specific and courteous salutation.

The various salutations are not interchangeable. With a little thought, you should find it easy to use the right one.

Incidentally, more and more people in recent years are questioning the use of the word *Dear* at the beginning of the salutation. You may drop it if you like. Most readers won't even notice it's missing if the rest of the letter is warm and courteous, and of course, if the letter is cold, *Dear* will not make it warmer. But do not drop the entire salutation—just the word *Dear.* Also, avoid using off-beat salutations like *Good morning Mr. Wilton.*

What salutation when you can't tell whether you are writing a man or woman? Find out. Again, a phone call will usually give you the information you need for an accurate and courteous salutation.

And what to do if you know it's a woman but are unsure whether she is *Miss* or *Mrs.?* Use the salutation *Ms.* (pronounced Mizz). In fact, most companies today instruct employees to use that for all women. It has gained respectability in recent years and, after all, we don't have separate titles for married and single men. (See page 84.)

The Opening Sentence. Many people use a cliché opening. That is, some well-known group of words used routinely to convey an implied meaning. Misguided writers often use these for convenience—*as substitutes for thinking of an individual message for each letter.* Such openings have all the sparkle of a bureaucratic form letter, and they make your letter sound like one. (Indeed, these clichés are most common in form letters, where the motive is often to be as general as possible, so the same wording will fit as many situations as possible.)

Try to avoid opening sentences containing such standard clichés as *in response to,* or *with reference to,* or *in accordance with,* or *relative to.* They are dull and overworked and suggest that you didn't put much work or thought into your opening. They have all the originality of a rubber stamp, and project the image that the writer is a rubber stamp with arms and legs. Here is an example of a typical cliché opening:

Mr. Matwood,

In response to your letter of February 19 relative to leasing office equipment, the Internal Revenue Service regulations on this point are complex. The technical differences between purchasing and leasing are not always clearly defined, and whether IRS considers your transaction a lease or purchase can be of tremendous importance in determining your tax rate.

Frankly, we doubt if there would be any advantage to. . . .

Here is that same letter again, but this time opening with a thoughtful, original statement that applies specifically to this situation.

Mr. Matwood,

Thank you for your letter of February 19 questioning whether you should lease or buy office equipment.

The Internal Revenue Service regulations on this point are complex. The technical differences between purchasing and leasing are not always clearly defined, and whether IRS considers your transaction a lease or purchase can be of tremendous importance in determining your tax rate.

Frankly, we doubt if there would be any advantage to. . . .

People who defend those cliché openings at the beginnings of letters do so on the grounds that the beginning should give a briefing of past correspondence. That kind of briefing may be useful (although it isn't always necessary), but, in fact, if you do want a briefing at the beginning, notice (above) that the individually thought out opening gives a far better, more informative briefing than the automatic opening in the first version of the letter to Mr. Matwood.

About Dictation

In the world of Writing Process 2000, dictation is almost a part of history, but for the occasional user it deserves some mention.

In terms of the quality of the finished writing, most business men and women write best when they do their own drafting—either in longhand or by typing their own. They do somewhat worse dictating to a secretary, and worst of all dictating to a machine. Why does dictation produce poor writing? It is certainly the fastest way to write, and it encourages conversational style, which should improve most people's writing. *The main trouble with dictation is that it deprives the writer's brain of something to look at.*

Remember, Chapter 8 demonstrated with the A-B-C Experiment (page 120) that it is impossible to organize your ideas well unless you can see them. Therefore, *outline first—even for the simplest letter—before you turn on the dictating machine.* Or, as one dictation equipment manufacturer put it: *Before turning on machine, make sure brain is engaged.*

Should you dictate punctuation, or let the secretary insert the punctuation marks? Generally, the writer knows better what effect he or she is trying to create with words and punctuation marks, and therefore should be better able to decide which ones should be used, and where they should go. The trouble is, secretaries usually know the rules of punctuation better. A sensible attitude seems to be: Whoever is most qualified should be in charge. Be sure, however, the two of you agree in advance.

By the way, invite secretaries or typists to contribute their talent to your writing. Encourage them to suggest better ways of saying things; you will have better writing and better employee relations. But caution: Other people should not make changes without discussing them with you first. If you were terribly unclear—and all of us are sometimes—another person might misinterpret and say the wrong thing in trying to clarify.

CHAPTER 9

REVIEW

How alert were you? All of these important points were discussed in the chapter you just read. You should be able to answer them all. If you cannot, it's in your interest to look them up.

What three important benefits do subject headings give the reader in reports?

____

____

They also help you, the writer. How?

____

____

What earlier aid should guide you in using headings? ______________

How does it guide you? ______________________

____

Headings should stand out. If you cannot use heavy type, make them stand out by:

____

____

How wide should margins be? ______________________

Describe the current advice on paragraph length.

____

____

If a report contains graphics, where should they generally appear?

____

How can you add emphasis to written words and phrases, similar to the way you add emphasis by raising your voice when talking?

____

When should you use each of these salutations in letters?

Dear (Name), ______

Dear Sir, ______

Gentlemen, ______

*What should one **not** expect when reviewing or editing the writing of others?*

______

"A watchdog that barks at every squirrel isn't very useful."

—Elliot Ness

CHAPTER 10

Reviewing and Editing the Writing of Others

First, let's say that the subordinate's writing, like any other professional skill, is certainly the manager's business. But writing is more difficult to evaluate than most other job skills, because there are no quick or precise ways to measure quality—no performance standards. And, because the writing in an office environment is so visible, many bosses have strong feelings about it and seem to become self-appointed experts. They may not always be right, and this can cause trouble. Some guidelines, therefore, are important.

In evaluating the writing of others, people often make a predictable mistake: They assume the best way to write anything is the way *they* would have written it. That attitude is unwise and may cause poor employee relations. A basic truth: There may be several ways to write anything, all equally good. *Even though the manager may be the better writer, then, it's unreasonable to expect that someone else should write a thing the way he or she would have written it.*

Another common mistake when managing other people's writing is to change things just for change's sake. For example, why change "A number of our representatives . . ." to "*Many* of our representatives"? True, that change makes the writing a bit shorter, but it is too minor to make *in other people's writing.* Again, it is poor employee relations, because it stifles initiative. Never give employees a chance to call you a nit-picker. How many times have we all heard people say, "*They're going to change everything anyhow, so what's the sense of trying to do a good job the first time?*" Sometimes that accusation is justified.

When we review someone else's writing, a wise attitude seems to be: "I'm a watchdog; my job is to ensure that what goes out meets our standards." A really wise watchdog should rejoice, however, if it isn't necessary to bark. A wise manager should rejoice if an employee's work is so good it needs little or no supervision.

Still, there are some things a reviewer has a right to expect. **Here is a six-point checklist for evaluating someone else's writing:**

- Is the content correct?
- Are the words clear and precise?

- Are the ideas divided properly into sentences?
- Is the conclusion at the beginning?
- Is the tone courteous?
- Are there headings to help the reader?

If the answer to these questions is yes, the writing should pass, and the reviewer should rejoice. But what happens when you must honestly conclude that the writing is not good enough?

A surprising number of managers or reviewers rewrite it themselves. This is unwise, for two reasons. First, if something is poorly written the boss may misinterpret and say the wrong thing in trying to clarify it. Second, rewriting their work does not help the weak writers. If their letters and reports need rewriting, the reviewer can help most by pointing out exactly what is wrong, and how to correct it. Are sentences too long? Words too complex? Is the organization weak? This kind of feedback—guidance from the manager—is necessary if the subordinate is to improve. Both will benefit; the subordinate will learn to improve an important professional skill, and the boss will need to spend less time editing and rewriting in the future.

Very minor editing and revising may not require discussion with the writer. But if changes are so extensive they reveal a basic writing deficiency, the manager should not correct the writing but should teach the writer. This may be one of the greatest favors he or she can do for an employee. The cruelest thing would be to list this deficiency in a written performance review without first trying to make help available.

Review of the outline. This is most useful for long reports, and it's surprising that many employers do not require it. Some companies call this the *pre-editorial* review. Often a lot of work goes wasted because a writer learns *after* writing that the approach taken was not what the manager wanted.

For project directors, reviewers, or others who have any influence in a report, approving the outline should be as important as the finished writing. Then, if they can help improve the overall approach, or want some other approach, the writer learns of it in advance, and the finished writing needs review only for editorial style—basic clarity. And that is exactly the way it should be.

Always remember, whether it is your writing or someone else's, that language is just a communications tool—a living tool of a living society. Your goal as a writer is to tell as much as possible, as accurately and clearly as possible, in as little reading as possible. That is the only purpose for which cultures create language. It is the only reason you write.

The Trouble With Jargon

Jargon is the specialized vocabulary of a particular profession. When used legitimately, it is a kind of shorthand, allowing people in that profession to express complex ideas in a few words. But it has a major disadvantage: Only people in that profession can understand it.

Further trouble comes from the fact that jargon is also a status symbol; for this reason, professions often create specialized terms when none are necessary.

What does the doctor mean by *topical* dressings? Are they dressings related to a topic? Or are they just *top* dressings? (Where else would they go?)

When lawyers discontinue a legal action, why do they say it has been *continued?* Why does the meaning of the term *quiet enjoyment* have nothing to do with either quiet or enjoyment? (It's a property term meaning *uninterrupted use.*) Lawyers argue that such phrases are "terms of art" and have specific meanings in court. But courts do not mandate their use. Plain English would be just as legal, and it would be more understandable to those of us who are governed by the laws.

It does not make sense to broadcast on a wavelength the person at the other end cannot receive—if you care to communicate.

CHAPTER 11

WHAT COMPUTERS CAN AND CAN'T DO FOR WRITERS

They are the most significant technological development of our time, but can computers write for us? No, they cannot. Will they in the future? Not likely.

No computer manufacturers or program publishers are making such claims.

Computers can do many things that are a joy to writers. They allow us to make changes quickly and easily, and they reduce the need to retype a whole letter or report, and proofread again, each time a small change is made. They can measure the size of words and sentences. They can warn if we use a word that's considered dangerous or commonly misused. And they can assemble letters—even large reports—from standard paragraphs held in storage; you just fill in the variable information. But someone still has to write these standard paragraphs. Some computer companies claim their systems can correct grammar, but even these modest claims seem exaggerated.

What about spelling? Yes, even inexpensive word processing programs can warn you of misspelled words and offer to correct each one with a single keystroke. Can you relax, then, smug with the confidence that you will never, ever again send out a letter with a typing error? Well, not really. Even in spelling, artificial intelligence has severe limitations. The computer warns you only if your misspelling, or other typing error, creates a *non-word.* If, for example, you type *noj* instead of *now,* the display will send you a danger signal, because *noj* is not on the program's approved word list. But if you type *not* instead of *now,* the computer will never blink an eye, because *not* is an approved word. That may reverse your meaning (*Our company can not. . . .* instead of *Our company can now. . . .*), but you will get no help from the electrons. It seems, then, for now anyhow, you will still have to proofread.

The real advantage computers offer writers is that revisions are so easy. The typist just replaces the words you change, and the printer gives you a new copy. Retyping the whole report is a thing of the past, and so is proofreading it again. As a result, writers can pamper themselves by making changes they might not have made in the past—second draft, third, tenth draft if they feel it is necessary—improvements they would not have made before because retyping would have been too much work.

All of these compu-luxuries fall far, far short of writing, however. *You* must still go through the same thinking process (the WHAT) and language process (the HOW), to give the computer something it can help you correct.

Will computers ever write for us? If writing is one's thinking put on paper, a better way of asking that question might be: Will computers ever think for us?

Would we want them to?

INDEX

A

Abstract:
- length of, 104
- reports, 104
- when to write, 105–106

Acronyms, 125
Active voice, 33–37
Address block, letters, 140
and, beginning sentences with, 52–53, 60
Antecedents, 55
Appendixes:
- reports, 105

Arranging information, 108, 112
Attention line, 140

B

Blind spots, 16
- finding/correcting, 38

Boldface, 140
Brevity, how important, 56–57
Bullets, 140
Bureaucratic writing style, 65–66
but, beginning sentences with, 52–53, 60
by whom information, and passive voice, 34–35

C

Chairman, sexist nature of title, 83
Charts, 139–140
- and appendixes, 105

Chesterfield, Earl of, 3
Churchill, Winston, 11, 34, 54
Clarity, 1–89
- and brevity, 56–57
- and conversational style, 37–38
- and jargon, 11–12
- mention people, 36–37
- passive voice verbs, avoiding, 33–37, 47
- principles of, 9–21, 33–41
- and professional words, 11–12
- repeated words, 54–56
- revising your writing, 38–39
- and sentence length, 14–20
- and small words, 11
- and your attitude toward choice of words, 10–11

Clichés, 54–55
- opening sentences as, 141–142

Clustering, 126
Coleridge, Samuel Taylor, 8
Commas, and quotation marks, 68
Computers, 149–150
Conclusion:
- length of, 104–105
- placing at the end, 101
- placing first, 100–101, 112–114

Conclusion (*continued*):
repeating, 100–101
reports, 104–105, 107
when to write, 105–106
Connectives (conjunctions), 52–53, 61
Conversational style, 37–38, 49

D

Deadlines, and planning, 120–121
Descarte, René, 3
Detail, 72, 127
Dictation, 142–143
Discussion:
length of, 105
reports, 105
Disney, Walt, Studios, 13
Drawings, 139–140

E

Editing other people's writing, 147–148
Ego satisfaction, and overcomplicated language, 7
Elevator door statement, 97
Elongated Yellow Fruit Sickness, 54
Emphasis, 54
adding, 140
in proportion to importance, 108
Expository writing, 94–96
elevator door statement, 97
five W's of journalism, 98–103
format reports, format for, 104–106
goals of, 97
Inverted Pyramid structure, 97–107
organizing, 95, 99

F

facilitate, 10
False start, importance of, 121–123
FALSE START outline, 123–124
FebRUary, 41
Fiore, Quentin, iv
First-choice words, 54–55
Fisherman Who Had Nobody to Go Out in His Boat with Him, The (Maxwell), 12–13
Five W's of journalism, 98–103
Flashback technique, 105*fn*
Formal reports, format for, 104–106
Four factorial pattern, 120
Freud, Sigmund, 32

G

Girl, referring to grown woman as, 83
Gobbledygook, 65–66
Grammar:
importance of, 55
rules of, 51–56
Graphics, 139–140
and appendixes, 105
Gunning, Robert, 75

H

He, 81–82
Headings, 135–138
reports, 108
Hemingway, Ernest, 118
Hippopotamus joke, 126
Huxley, Aldous, 80

I

I and *we,* interchanging, 37
Iambic pentameter, 13

Ideas:
buried, 17
dividing into sentences, 16
multiple, in long sentences, 15–16
and word clusters, 14–15
Image, 6
Imagery, 12
Impersonal tone, 36–37
indicated, 10
Information clusters, size of, 14–15
Introduction:
length of, 104
reports, 104
Inverted Pyramid structure, 97–107
disadvantage of, 106–107
Italics, 140

J

Jargon, 148
and clarity, 11–12
Job descriptions, sexism in, 82–83
Job titles, sexism in, 83–84
Journalism, five W's of, 98–103

K

Key word phrases, outlining with, 126

L

Ladies, referring to grown woman as, 83
Language:
changes in, 51
purpose of, 4
rules of grammar, 51–56
special, 11–12
Language workload, 70–71
Large words:
and clarity, 11–12
and resistance to understanding, 70
Lazy thinking, and overcomplicated language, 6–7
Leadership, and image, 6
Legal writing, 75–76
Letters, 140–142
address block, 140
dictation, 142–143
opening sentence, 141–142
salutation, 141
subject line, 141
Long sentences:
buried ideas in, 17
difficulty in reading, 15
meat cleaver technique, 16–17
multiple ideas in, 15–16
and subordinate clauses, 17

M

McLuhan, Marshall, iv
Man words, 82
Maxwell, William, 12–13
Measuring readability, 67
Meat cleaver technique, 16
Melville, Herman, iv, 92
Mind dump, 99
Mind mapping, 125–126
Misguidance, and overcomplicated language, 6
Moby Dick (Melville), 71–72
Ms., 84

N

Narrative writing, 95–96
Ness, Elliot, 146
Noble English Sentence, The, 33–34
Nonrestrictive clauses and phrases, rule of, 16

Nonsexist writing guidelines, 81–84
he, 81–82
job descriptions, 82–83
job titles that identify sex, avoiding, 83
man words, 82
Ms., 84
Nouns, turning verbs into, 57
Numbers, spelling out, 12

O

Official tone, 74
Opening sentence, letters, 141–142
Order of information, 108, 112
Organization checklist, 107–108
Organizing the ideas, 93
Orwell, George, 134
Outlining, 122, 123–127
detail, 127
FALSE START outline, 123–124
hints for, 126
and key word phrases, 126
mind mapping, 125
reviewing, 148
Roman numerals and, 123
time required for, 126–127
and word/sentence skill, 126
Overcomplicated language, 4–7
reasons for use of, 6–7
Oversimplified writing, 5
Overview statement:
importance of, 96
reports, 107
See also Conclusion

P

paradigms, 10
Paragraphs:
length of, 55–56, 137
structuring, 137
parameters, 10
Passive voice verbs:
appropriate use of, 35, 46
avoiding, 33–37
and *by whom* information, 34–35, 45
changing to active, 33–37, 44
and dull writing, 35
past tense compared to, 35
recognizing, 35–36
and the writing of procedures, 34–35
Penguin joke, 7
Pentameter, iambic, 13
People, referring to, 36
Periods, 16, 18
in legal writing, 75–76
and quotation marks, 68
Persuasion, 6
Photographs, 139–140
Planning, 119–127
and deadlines, 120–121
false start, importance of, 121–123
outlines, 123–127
Plurals, avoiding sexist writing by switching to, 82
Poe, Edgar Allan, 13
Polysyllables, 70
figuring percentage of, 71
Pope, Alexander, 148
Pratt's Law, 72
Preeditorial review, 148
Preliminary sections, writing, 105–106
Prepositions, ending sentences with, 53–54
Pre-writing, *see* Planning
Professional words, and clarity, 11–12
Professional writers:
knowing your reader, 9
as teachers, 7
Pronoun antecedents, rule of, 15–16
Pronouns, 55
Punctuation:
dictating, 143
inside/outside quotation marks, 68

Pyramid, *see* Inverted Pyramid structure

R

Radiant thinking, 125–126
Raven, The (Poe), 13
Readability, measuring, 67–77
  language workload, 71
  Readability Index, 71–72
  and sentence difficulty, 70
  steps in, 71
  strengths/weaknesses, analyzing, 72
  word difficulty, 70
Readability formulas, limitation of, 72–74
Reader, identifying, 9
Reading process, 68–69
Recommendations:
  length of, 105
  reports, 105
Repeating words, 54–56
Reviewing other people's writing, 147–148
Revising, 38–39
Rhythm, 12
Romeo and Juliet (Shakespeare), 13
Rule of nonrestrictive clauses and phrases, 16
Rule of pronoun antecedents, 15–16
Rules of grammar, 51–56

S

Salutation, letters, 141
Scientific writing, 76
Selling, and image, 6
Sentence difficulty, and readability, 70
Sentence length, and clarity, 14–20
Sentences:
  beginning with *and* or *but,* 52–53
  dividing ideas into, 16
  ending with a preposition, 53–54
  paragraph length, 55–56
  periods, 18
Sequence of information, 108, 112
Sexist writing, *see* Nonsexist writing guidelines
Shakespeare, William, 13, 51
Shaw, George Bernard, 50
Short sentences, 16
  combining, 18
  impact of, 16, 21
  overuse of, 18
Size/length:
  abstract, 104
  appendixes, 105
  conclusion, 104–105
  discussion, 105
  introduction, 104
  recommendations, 105
  sentences, 14–18
  summary, 104
  title, 104
  words, 10–14
Slang, 4
Small words:
  beauty added by, 12–13
  and clarity, 10, 11
  and resistance to understanding, 70
Snow job, masking weak material with, 7
Speed of communication process, 5
Spell checkers, 149
Stanhope, Philip Dormer, 3
Street talk, 4
Style:
  children's, 3
  conversational, 37
  definition of, 3
  moderate, 4
  overcomplicated, 4
Subheading, reports, 108
Subject line, letters, 140
Subject-object relationship, 34

Subject workload, 71
Subordinate clauses, 17
subsequently, 10
Summary:
  length of, 104
  reports, 104
  when to write, 105–106
Summary statements, 100–101
Synonyms, 55, 62–63

T

Tables, 139–140
  and appendixes, 105
Taboos, The three, 51
Tenses, mixing, 55
Tetrameter, 13
Thesaurus, and word choices, 58
Third person, 36
  he/she, 82
Three factorial pattern, 120
Title:
  length of, 104
  reports, 104
  when to write, 105–106
to be, 35–36
Tone, 74
Trochaic tetrameter, 13

U

unit, 55

V

Verbs:
  active vs. passive, 33–37
  as action words, 57
  tenses, mixing, 55
  transitive, 33
  turning into nouns, 57
Vocabulary:
  and legal writing, 75
  and scientific writing, 76

W

Wasted words, eliminating, 56–57, 64
We and *I*, interchanging, 37
Weak material, concealing with overcomplicated language, 7
White space, importance of, 136
Who, What, Where, When, Why, 98–103
Word difficulty, and readability, 70
Words:
  choosing, 10–14
  first-choice, 54–55
  large, 11–12
  man, 82
  professional, 11–12
  repeated, 54–56
  small, 11
  wasted, eliminating, 56–57, 64
Workload:
  reader, 68
  word/sentence relationship, 68
Wrap-up statements, 100–101
Writerbrain/readerbrain relationship, 68
Writing:
  bureaucratic, 65–66
  editing other people's, 147–148
  expository, 94–96
  legal, 75–76
  narrative, 95–96
  nonsexist, 81–84
  oversimplified, 5
  reasons for, 39
  revising, 38–39
  scientific, 76
  vs. phone call, 39
Writing styles, 3–4
  of others, examining/learning from, 14

Notes

Notes

Notes

Notes